Credible Checklists and Quality Questionnaires

Credible Checklists and Quality Questionnaires

Questionnaires

A User-Centered Design Method

Chauncey Wilson

AMSTERDAM • BOSTON • HEIDELBERG • LONDON
NEW YORK • OXFORD • PARIS • SAN DIEGO
SAN FRANCISCO • SINGAPORE • SYDNEY • TOKYO
Morgan Kaufmann is an imprint of Elsevier

ELSEVIER

Acquiring Editor: Meg Dunkerley
Development Editor: Heather Scherer
Project Manager: Mohana Natarajan

Morgan Kaufmann is an imprint of Elsevier
225 Wyman Street, Waltham, MA 02451, USA

First published 2013

British Library Cataloguing-in-Publication Data
A catalogue record for this book is available from the British Library

Library of Congress Cataloging-in-Publication Data
A catalog record for this book is available from the Library of Congress

ISBN: 978-0-12-410392-4

For information on all MK publications
visit our website at *www.mkp.com*

CONTENTS

INTRODUCTION

This book begins with a brief description of the essential, but often overlooked checklist method. Checklists are used for many things in user-centered design (UCD), such as verifying that we are prepared for a usability test, that we have asked the critical questions during field interviews, and that we have followed best practices in the design of questionnaires. The literature on human factors is replete with research on checklists, but a review of the UCD literature reveals little about what makes a good checklist. Chapter 1 provides some basic principles and practical tips for creating good checklists for UCD activities.

Because much of what we do as UCD professionals is ask questions about users, tasks, context, artifacts, and anything else that might affect the success or failure of our products and services, Chapter 2 focuses on the design of questionnaires and surveys. Designing a valid and reliable questionnaire is difficult. Among other issues, questionnaire designers have to ask themselves many tough questions about phrasing, the ordering of questions, and the scales that are used to provide answers. Failing to address these issues thoughtfully can have a major impact on how people answer the questions, to the point of limiting the usefulness and validity of the survey.

Clearly, a questionnaire is a complex user interface (UI) that you cannot just "throw together" and send out to customers. Questionnaire design is part science and part art. The second chapter in this book covers some general principles of questionnaire design and describes a clear process for creating useful and usable UCD questionnaires. Chapter 2 can be viewed as a checklist for questionnaire and survey designers. At the end of book, an appendix provides information on some well-known usability questionnaires that might be useful for readers of this book.

Checklists

Four generations after the first aviation checklists went into use, a lesson is emerging: checklists seem able to defend anyone, even the experienced, against failure in many more tasks than we realized. They provide a kind of cognitive net. They catch mental flaws inherent in all of us—flaws of memory and attention and thoroughness. And because they do, they raise wide, unexpected possibilities.
Gawande, Atul, from The Checklist Manifesto: How to Get Things Right *(p. 48)*

AlternateNames: Audit, inspection

Related Methods: Heuristic evaluation, user interface inspection, participant observation, questionnaire, structured interview, semi-structured interview, style guide

OVERVIEW OF CHECKLISTS

Checklists are predefined lists of guidelines, tasks, questions, or other items against which products, processes, behaviors, tasks, user interface (UI) components, and so on, are compared. Checklists are often condensed style guides, detailed procedural guides (useful when procedures are too complex or lengthy to memorize), or other core source documents. Checklists can range in size from a single word mnemonic (e.g., "AEIOU") to a page or two of Yes/No items to something as long as an entire book, manual, or construction plans for a skyscraper. You can think of a checklist, whatever the size, as a risk-reduction tool; the bigger the risks, the more time you need to invest in the design and testing of your checklist. As Atul Gawande notes in his book, *The checklist manifesto: How to get things right* (Metropolitan books, 2009), checklists help prevent many simple errors and also prompt colleagues as they work through complex tasks or problems.

Weblink

Web design checklists http://www.smashingmagazine.com/2009/06/29/45-incredibly-useful-web-design-checklists-and-questionnaires/ (or search for "web design checklist smashing magazine cameron chapman")

●●●——

The National Checklist Program for IT Products

The National Institute of Standards and Technologies (NIST) of the US Department of Commerce published a document titled "National Checklist Program for IT Products—Guidelines for Checklist Users and Developers" (Quinn, Souppaya, Cook, & Scarfone, 2011). Although the focus of this document is on security configuration checklists that are used to reduce the risk that IT systems will be compromised by hackers, it contains useful information on how to design and evaluate checklists. Some of the lessons in this document (such as testing a checklist in an operational environment, identifying explicitly the skill level needed to use a checklist, and including troubleshooting information) are useful for the development of many types of checklists. You can find this document by searching for "Security Configuration Checklists Program for IT Products: Guidance for Checklists Users and Developers."

———

The purpose of this chapter is to provide some practical insights into using and creating checklists for user-centered design (UCD) activities. It can be very helpful to review existing checklists, both to determine whether a custom checklist is required for your project and to provide a feel for what makes a good checklist. Here are some examples of checklists that you can access on the web to get a sense of the range of available UCD checklists:

- *Usability Testing Checklist*: This type of checklist is a list of reminders about what a person must do to plan and conduct a successful usability test. An example of a usability testing checklist for participants with disabilities (Henry, 2007) can be found at http://www. uiaccess.com/accessucd/ut_checklist.html. Many books on UCD methods contain valuable checklists that can prevent errors, support learning, and provide memory aids about what to look for when evaluating a product or service.
- *The Voluntary Product Accessibility Template® (VPAT®)*: This checklist is used to evaluate a product against the accessibility requirements of Section 508 of the Rehabilitation Act. In the United States, the VPAT is used by governmental agencies to assess the accessibility of products. The VPAT checklist can be found at http://www.itic.org/public-policy/accessibility.

- *Checklist for Questionnaire Design*: This checklist provides best practices on how to design questions and self-completion questionnaires. For an online example, see Appendix 1 at http://www.dataunitwales.gov.uk/SharedFiles/Download.aspx?pageid = 79&fileid = 447 &mid = 459. You can also find this document by searching on "a guide to questionnaire design dataunitwales."

The UCD literature is filled with examples of procedural, design, and evaluation checklists (Drury, 2012; Stanton, Salmon, Walker, Baber, & Jenkins, 2005), but there is little discussion in the UCD domain about what makes a "good" checklist. This chapter describes different types of checklists, procedures for developing checklists, and some general guidance on style and formatting.

Types of Checklists
Following are some common types of checklists that are used in UCD activities.

Do-Confirm/Read-Do Checklists
Gawande (2009) describes two general types of checklists. The first type is the *do-confirm* checklist where a person completes an activity from memory and then, at some "pause point" reviews the checklist to ensure that all critical steps in a task have been completed. A second type of checklist, called *read-do*, requires that a person read an item in a checklist and then perform that item in sequence. When an item is complete, the person checks it off and goes to the next step. The read-do style of checklist is much like following a recipe (if you are an amateur chef you know how important it is to follow recipe steps in order).

Procedure Checklists
The procedure checklist provides a list of tasks or steps required to complete a procedure successfully. You might, for example, create a checklist of the tasks required for setting up a usability test session and use that checklist after each session to make sure that you have cleared the cache, have all your forms ready, have money for incentives, and know the name and background of the next participant. Procedural checklists serve as concrete reminders of what tasks need to be performed, what information is needed for a task, and what order a series of tasks needs to be performed. Procedural checklists are meant to eliminate errors such as forgetting a critical step in a task and doing

steps in the wrong order. To evaluate your procedure checklist, you might use the following questions:

- Are all the necessary steps listed?
- Is a particular step necessary?
- Are the steps in the checklist in the most efficient order?
- Does the checklist deal with alternative paths (if A, then this...; if B, then that...)?
- Will the terminology be understood by the range of expected users?
- Can this checklist be given to a new colleague to use without any training?
- Is each step described in enough detail for the range of anticipated users?
- Is there a clear statement of success for each task?
- Does the list clearly indicate when other data, tools, or materials are required to complete a step? For example, did the checklist let you know that you needed a particular kind of battery for the audio system in your usability laboratory?
- Does the checklist provide troubleshooting information for steps in a procedure where "trouble" is likely?
- Does the checklist identify how to send feedback to the checklist owner?

Procedure checklists often receive an initial evaluation before official use, but there should also be a plan for iterative feedback and evaluation to continuously improve the checklist.

Evaluation Checklists
Evaluation checklists are tools for assessing a product or service against a set of principles, best practices, or specific criteria (Brykczynski, 1999). This type of checklist can be used for software, usability, document, process, or other types of inspections. An example of this type of checklist is: Usability Techniques: Heuristic Evaluation—A System Checklist, at http://www.stcsig.org/usability/topics/articles/he-checklist.html.

Evaluation checklists may provide different levels of explanatory information depending on assumptions about the expertise of the inspector/evaluator. If the checklist is for a person without a great deal of experience or expertise, then you might provide more details about the checklist item and perhaps examples to support understanding. Take, for example, two items from the heuristic evaluation of UIs

Table 1.1 Sample Items for an Evaluation Checklist						
Feature	Heuristic	Yes	No	N/A	Not Sure	Considerations/Examples
	Be consistent	☐	☐	☐	☐	• Capitalization and alignment are used consistently and follow corporate guidelines. • Layouts follow a grid style. • Similar tasks use common interaction patterns (e.g., there is a common search pattern). • Labels use consistent language. • Terminology is consistent across the feature or product. • The use of color is consistent across the product.
	Provide shortcuts	☐	☐	☐	☐	• All features can be accessed through the keyboard. • Pop-up menus are used to minimize mouse movement. • Provide bulk operations for tasks (e.g., allow someone to choose 100 photos and put in a tag). • Allow users to create macros for repetitive actions. • Allow users to access nested information quickly.

(Nielsen & Molich, 1990): "Be consistent" and "Provide shortcuts." An UCD practitioner with 20 years of experience may have a deep understanding of consistency—a complicated concept (Wilson, 2009)—and shortcuts, so those two items might be sufficient memory aids. However, a new graduate student in human–computer interaction (HCI) may need more information. Table 1.1 shows the two heuristic evaluation items with additional considerations and examples to help less experienced users. Note that there is a "Not Sure" option because new practitioners may not be sure whether a feature is "consistent." If this checklist was online, the bullets in the last column could be links to a pattern library or style guide to provide even more details.

Feature Checklist
A feature checklist (Edgerton, Draper, & Barton, 1993) has a list of product features that are used to cue a participant or interviewer. The general format is a long list of features or UI components with several columns for specific questions (e.g., Do you use this feature? How is this feature used? How often is it used? How usable is the feature?).

A feature checklist can be used to gather data on the frequency of use or importance of features or commands in a system that has no built-in logging capabilities or to gather qualitative data that cannot be easily logged. The results of the feature checklist could be used, for example, as input into a task analysis, although you would want to validate your data with other task analysis methods. This type of checklist can suffer from recall distortion (the tendency to revise memories of past usage patterns) if the features are rarely used or have not been used much recently. For example, asking a person in the United States questions about features in an income tax program used months earlier is not be recommended because the passage of time renders the data suspect.

Behavior Sampling Checklist

This type of checklist contains a list of behaviors or activities that the investigator or participant checks off during a specified time period. Behavior sampling checklists can be used during participant observation to record what people are doing at specified intervals. You might use a behavior sampling checklist to indicate what and when behaviors should be recorded during a laboratory study or field visit. If you were observing people at a field site, you might create a behavior sampling checklist to focus on the behaviors of interest.

●●●———————————————————————————

Sample of an Activity Classification Scheme from the US Bureau of Labor Statistics

The US Bureau of Labor Statistics (BLS) has an extensive activity classification scheme with 26 pages of time use categories and examples. In the "Socializing, Relaxing, and Leisure" category, there are 14 activities of time use:

01 Relaxing, thinking
02 Tobacco and drug use
03 Television and movies (not religious)
04 Television (religious)
05 Listening to the radio
06 Listening to/playing music (not radio)
07 Playing games
08 Computer use for leisure (excluding games)
09 Arts and crafts as a hobby
10 Collecting as a hobby
11 Hobbies, except arts and crafts and collecting
12 Reading for personal interest
13 Writing for personal interest
99 Relaxing and leisure

The BLS statistics categories can be a useful starting point for developing behavior sampling categories for field or observational studies.

One of the key issues with a behavior sampling checklist is choosing the appropriate level of granularity of the checklist items; that is, how much detail do you need for your research? For example, if you are observing people using a mobile device, what level of activity will support your research goals? The activities items could be at a high level, such as the following:

- Chat with a colleague
- Make a phone call
- Answer a phone call
- Send e-mail
- Answer e-mail
- Use a browser
- Use an application

If your research requires more detail, you could take these high-level items and break them down further, for example:

- Use a browser:
  - Google®
  - Wikipedia
  - Access to business application
  - Newsreader
  - Pinterest
  - Usability blogs
  - Other
- Use an application:
  - WolframAlpha®
  - Evernote®
  - iChalkboard
  - Numbers®
  - Autodesk® SketchBook® Pro
  - iMockups
  - Other

How do take a behavior like "use a browser" and break it down further? If you have some data from logging studies that indicate the frequency of access to particular applications, you can use that to suggest new categories. If you are lacking your own empirical data, you can search for public sites that provide statistics on usage. You can also perform a preliminary survey or conduct some focus groups or brainstorming sessions for breaking categories into subcategories. There may be "surprise" behaviors so any checklist needs an "Other" category and some way to include the unexpected (which you can later incorporate into an updated checklist).

If you are creating a behavior sampling checklist, you need to consider several questions:

- Can you capture all the behaviors or activities necessary for your research on the checklist that you created?
- Is your behavior sampling checklist laid out so that you have room to write supporting notes?
- Is the level of detail adequate for your purposes? For example, would an item such as "Reads documentation" be sufficient? Would you want to know if the person is reading online Help versus reading the user's manual sitting on his/her desk or an e-mail from a technical expert in corporate support?
- Do you need to record the length of various activities? Are you noting activities that occur within particular intervals (say every one, five, ten, or fifteen minutes)?
- Do you need to know the precise beginning and ending times of activities?
- Can you deal with unusual but important activities that might occur? Is there a place on your behavior sampling checklist to accommodate "surprises"?

Consider a study of office behavior where you are sampling how people work together. You might have, for example, an exhaustive checklist crowded with categories that include the following:

- Face-to-face meetings
- Phone calls with more than one person
- Online discussion groups based on e-mail
- Blogs and wikis
- Videoconference
- Hallway meetings
- Food gatherings
- Beer bashes at the local pub on Friday nights
- Internal chat
- External chat

Even so, during the first hour of behavior sampling, you will likely observe a few forms of collaboration that you did not anticipate on your checklist:

- People post small adhesive notes on an "idea board" about possible requirements for future products and others add comments to the ideas.
- There is a weekly "pin-up" exercise where UI designs are pinned to a board and critiqued by anyone who wants to stop by.
- There is a large closet in the company where people can talk privately with a clinical psychologist who is paid to help with collaboration problems.

Activity Checklists

An activity checklist is meant to help UCD practitioners focus on important contextual factors that affect how a computer tool is used (Kaptelinin, Nardi, & Macaulay, 1999). The activity checklist is based on activity theory, a framework that stresses how human interaction (activities) can only be understood within a social and cultural context. The activity checklist can be used for early product design inquiries or later evaluation of a prototype or working product.

Entry/Exit Checklist

Checklists can be used to determine if product, service, or process is ready for submission, review, or release. In the software domain, you might use an entry checklist to determine whether a product is ready for a detailed usability inspection, or you might use an exit checklist to see if the product is ready for release to beta customers. Groups such as the User Experience Professionals Association (UXPA) and the Industrial Designers Society of America provide entry checklists for conference proposals and industrial design competitions. If you have left a job, you are probably familiar with the exit checklists that human resource groups use to ensure that your separation from an organization is thorough and efficient.

Research Checklist

This type of checklist can be used to determine if research is credible by evaluating methodology against commonly accepted standards. A research checklist can also be used as a guide for writing research papers (Wieringa, Condori-Fernandez, Daneva, Mutschler, & Pastor, 2012). It might include items dealing with the following:

- Motivation for the research
- Definition of a research topic
- Measurement specification
- Population of interest
- Sampling limitations
- Sources (funding, researchers' qualifications)
- Appropriateness of research methods
- Limitations of the study
- Common biases that might affect the results of a study
- Internal and external validity
- Data analysis methods

The research checklist can be used, for example, by graduate students who are asked to review articles or professionals who are reading literature to support product development.

WHEN SHOULD YOU USE A CHECKLIST?

You can use checklists when you need to do the following:

- Evaluate products or processes against a set of criteria, principles, or guidelines. For example, you might evaluate whether a UI follows platform and corporate appearance and interaction guidelines.
- Verify whether all the steps in a task have been completed properly. For example, you might use a checklist for the setup of a remote usability test comprised of many steps using multiple products with significant risks to credibility if the study goes awry.
- Provide a person with a mnemonic device to reduce recall errors and errors that might result from forgetting or distractions. For example, the checklist might be a set of standard questions that you want to ask each person participating in a series of field or contextual interviews.
- Provide reviewers of products with hints and recommendations for finding bugs or other types of defects (Brykczynski, 1999). For example, a list of common problems and usability principles can be useful during informal and formal design reviews.

Table 1.2 Phases of Development When Checklists Are Useful				
✓	✓	✓	✓	✓
Problem Definition	Requirements	Conceptual Design	Detailed Design	Implementation

- Record samples of various activities in a particular setting (often called "activity sampling"). If you are conducting observational studies, you might have a form where you can "check off" particular behaviors and later use the checklist to provide quantitative data on behavior. Observational studies, for example, require a systematic recording of behaviors, artifacts, interactions between people and systems, environments, people, and external events (Martin & Hanington, 2012). Checklists can be a useful method for codifying observations and making sure that important aspects are not overlooked.
- Assess the interrater reliability of observers or evaluators by comparing responses to the same checklist. If you have multiple observers for a usability test, for example, you can use a checklist to examine the consistency of their observations (this is a great teaching tool by the way).

Checklists can be used throughout the development process (Table 1.2), from problem definition to working product implementation and improvement, in different ways (Stanton et al., 2005).

You can use a checklist early in the design process as an aid in reviewing competitive products (the heuristic evaluation or feature checklists). Lee, Jin, and Ji (2011), for example, used a heuristic evaluation checklist that incorporated principles of appliance design to evaluate the usability of common home appliances. Later in the design process, you can use checklists for recruiting test participants, setting up field visits for beta interviews, or conducting a release audit to determine if the product is ready to ship to customers.

●●●————————————————————————————————

User Experience (UX) Release-Readiness Checklist

A UX release-readiness checklist is an exit document that indicates whether a particular set of product features provides an acceptable user experience. Here is a brief example of a release readiness checklist for a desktop software product:

☐   All features are accessible through the keyboard.

☐ There are no severity one or two usability bugs.
☐ The product meets Section 508 accessibility goals.
☐ The system provides safeguards for catastrophic loss of data.
☐ The system provides support for international date, time, and currency formats.
☐ Usability goals for satisfaction have been met.
☐ Usability goals for effectiveness (task success) have been met.
☐ Usability goals for learning have been met.
☐ Usability goals for efficiency have been met.

One political issue with release-readiness checklists is that they can cause great angst if the product team has not considered them from the beginning of the design. A release-readiness checklist should be part of the planning process and used to assess UX release readiness throughout development so there are no surprises when the product is ready to ship.

For a more extensive example of a UX release-readiness checklist based on some common usability heuristics (Pierotti, n.d.), see http://www.anst.uu.se/larsoest/uploads/Main/HeuristicEvalChecklist.pdf (or search using the keywords "Denise Pierotti stc heuristic evaluation checklist").

Table 1.3 illustrates the relative effort required, on average, to develop and use checklists. Many checklists require limited resources, however, if your checklist is used for high-risk situations, the resources required may increase considerably.

Checklists have both strengths and weaknesses that you should consider.

Strengths
Checklists have the following strengths:

- They are easy to administer and use. Many checklists simply require people to mentally or physically check an item.
- Less training is required than with other methods.
- The output produced by checklists is immediately useful.

Table 1.3 Relative Effort and Resources Required for Checklist Development and Use				
Overall Effort Required	Time for Planning and Conducting	Skills and Experience	Supplies and Equipment	Time for Data Analysis
▨☐☐☐☐	▨▨☐☐☐	▨▨☐☐☐	▨☐☐☐☐	▨☐☐☐☐

- They can serve as memory aids that remind people what to do or what to observe.
- Analysts have the flexibility to easily customize checklists by adding or removing sections or modifying items.

Weaknesses
Checklists have the following weaknesses:

- Compared to usability tests and other methods, checklists are a weak form of evaluation because they do not take context (fatigue, interruptions, and collaboration patterns) or environment (using a system in the rain or snow) into account—factors that might lead to overly positive evaluations.
- Physical or cognitive errors associated with the product are often not taken into account (Stanton et al., 2005).
- Checklists are often incomplete. For example, one early heuristic evaluation checklist had only 10 general principles against which products were to be evaluated. This small and general set covered some, but not all, aspects of product usability.
- The context of use (Stanton et al., 2005) is often not taken into account. For example, the use of a product such as a laptop computer in a military vehicle that is dodging obstacles and bullets may be quite different from the use of that same product inside a home in the suburbs of Boston.
- Checklists can be used to record observed problems or behaviors but not necessarily the sequence of events that led up to the problem or target behavior. Activity checklists, for example, capture the frequencies of behaviors or events but not always the workflow.
- Although checklists appear simple, understanding the checklist items may require training or domain experience. For example, the heuristic evaluation method uses the principle of "Match between system and the real world." You could include a brief explanation of what this means in the heuristic evaluation form, but this principle can involve many aspects of metaphor and mapping—complex topics that cannot be explained in a short checklist.
- They are often too general or too specific to be useful for products that are used in many contexts. "The product is consistent" is an example of a checklist item that is too general to be of much use. Consistency is a complex attribute, and, at a minimum, the question

should focus on specific types of consistency such as visual consistency, interaction consistency, icon consistency, and layout consistency.

Bevan and Macleod (1994) caution against the use of checklists as the only type of usability assessment because understanding the usability of a product or service often requires detailed knowledge of the users, tasks, environment, and other aspects of the context of use. You can create a checklist with great detail, but then the checklist becomes so specific that it may not work in different real-world settings. Evaluation checklists need to be used with other methods such as usability testing, user forums, bug reporting systems, and field testing.

PROCEDURES AND PRACTICAL ADVICE ON CHECKLISTS

This section describes how to create a useful and usable checklist.

Creating a New Checklist

To create a new checklist, follow these steps:

1. **State the goal for the checklist.** Be clear when you define the goal for your checklist. You might, for example, create a checklist to do the following:
   a. Evaluate a product or process for usability flaws. The goal here is to provide a reviewer with best practices, principles, and tips that support the finding of defects. Heuristic evaluation checklists support this goal.
   b. Evaluate a product to determine if it meets particular standards, guidelines, or quality metrics such as ISO compliance.
   c. Deal with an emergency or abnormal situation. A checklist for restarting the equipment in a usability laboratory after a power outage supports this goal.
   d. Record behaviors or activities.
   e. Remind yourself and others of procedures, questions, or topics that you need to consider. A checklist of standard questions that you should ask all your participants supports this goal.
   f. Verify that procedures have been followed in a prescribed order. A checklist of maintenance procedures on hardware or troubleshooting procedures for software supports this goal.
2. **Determine if there are any existing checklists that you can use as a model for your checklist.** If there are existing checklists related to

your goal, consider whether one of them can be modified to meet your needs. For example, if you want to conduct an inspection of collaboration software, you could search the ACM Digital Library (note that this is a paid service) (http://www.acm.org/dl.cfm) and look for an existing checklist like the one proposed by Baker, Greenberg, and Gutwin (2002, p. 98):

a. Heuristic 1: Provide the means for intentional and appropriate verbal communication.
b. Heuristic 2: Provide the means for intentional and appropriate gestural communication.
c. Heuristic 3: Provide consequential communication of an individual's embodiment.
d. Heuristic 4: Provide consequential communication of shared artifacts (i.e., artifact feed through).
e. Heuristic 5: Provide protection.
f. Heuristic 6: Manage the transitions between tightly coupled and loosely coupled collaboration.
g. Heuristic 7: Support people with the coordination of their actions.
h. Heuristic 8: Facilitate finding collaborators and establishing contact.

If you want to avoid paid services, you can do a Google® search using sets of key words such as "heuristic evaluation checklist" or "field study checklist usability." You will find examples of checklists that support different goals and use those checklists as inspiration.

If there is no existing checklist that can serve as a model, then you need to identify the main topics that your checklist will cover and the individual items under each topic. Developing a new checklist requires iterations of design and evaluation of the headings and items. Creating a new checklist is not a trivial task because of the following necessary tasks:

a. You have to understand the domain.
b. You must figure out what to include in the list and what to exclude.
c. You need to understand your checklist users to know how much detail or background will be needed for them to understand the intent of the checklist items (unless you are the sole user of the checklist).

3. **Involve all the people who are stakeholders.** When you design your checklist, make sure that you involve all the stakeholders who

might be affected. For example, if you were creating a checklist for "release readiness of a new software product" you would involve members of the entire product team—developers, UX colleagues, quality assurance engineers, trainers, product managers, and content specialists.

4. **Determine the form of the checklist.** The form might be influenced by environmental factors or other situational factors (e.g., you will be using a new cell phone while walking on the street during a mobile device observation study). Your checklist can take the following forms:

   a. A small laminated card
   b. A paper form
   c. An online web form
   d. A tablet or smartphone application
   e. An audio "form"
   f. A mnemonic that prompts recall of a set of items such as *FIOPP*, a mnemonic that represents four important things about tasks that you might want to ask: *f*requency, *i*mportance, *o*rder, and *p*ain *p*oints. Another mnemonic method for field studies is *AEIOU* (Martin & Hanington, 2012), which stands for *a*rtifacts, *e*nvironment, *i*nteractions, *o*bjects, and *u*sers. This mnemonic is a reminder about what categories of information should be recorded for ethnographic studies and contextual inquiry.

5. **Review best practices for the type of checklists that you are creating.** Some examples of best practices are listed throughout this chapter. There may be industry or organizational best practices for particular types of checklists. Some general best practices include the following:

   a. Create a title that conveys the objectives of the checklist.
   b. Use large bold headings to identify sections of the checklist.
   c. Group items in a logical order for your particular goals.
   d. Design the checklist so that it can fit on a single page for simple tasks. If your task is complex and you need a multipage form, consider issues such as repeating headers, subtitles for sections, and appropriate page breaks.
   e. Use a font size that allows readability under poor lighting conditions.
   f. Use a mix of lowercase and uppercase letters. Avoid all uppercase unless you want to make a strong point about a particular checklist item.

g. Design conditional statements (if A, then Step X; if B, then Step Y) so they are logically coherent and make sense to the checklist user. Test conditional statements with a sample of actual users to make sure that that they are clearly understood (Brykczynski, 1999; Burian, 2004).

6. **Choose or develop the individual checklist items based on the relevant usefulness and usability criteria.** Criteria to consider when you are developing checklist items include the following:

   a. *Relevance*: Are the questions relevant given stated user experience and business goals?

   b. *Generality/Granularity*: Your checklist might have an item on a release-readiness checklist that asks "Does this product support Section 508 accessibility guidelines?"—a very general question. Early in design, you might want more specific checklist items such as the following that focus on individual aspects of accessibility:

      • All images use ALT tags
      • All charts provide text alternatives
      • All features are accessible through the keyboard
      • Audio and video files provide captioning or a text version
      • There is a logical tab order
      • Contrast ratio between text and background meets accessibility guidelines.

   c. *Consistency of terminology and appearance*: Do not use synonyms for the same thing. Minimize the use of abbreviations and acronyms.

   d. *Inclusiveness*: Are you capturing the key items?

   e. *Style of the items (question versus declarative statement)*: Use a consistent style for the items.

   f. *Understandability to your users*: How well do they understand the domain and the specific items on the checklist? Consider having some "novice" users review and comment on your items.

   g. *Length of items and the length of the checklist itself*: The length of a checklist will depend on the complexity of a task. If there are many items in a checklist (say more than 10), consider breaking the items into subgroups. Review each items for unneeded words that do not add to the clarity or memorability of the item.

●●●
_____

Pause Points in Checklists

Dr. Atul Gawande and Dan Boorman (Gawande, 2009) collaborated on a checklist of checklists that suggested that there be "fewer than 10 items per pause point" where a pause point was a place where a DO-CONFIRM checklist (a checklist where you do a set of tasks, then confirm that you did all the tasks correctly) was used. You can find the latest "Checklist of Checklists" at http://www.projectcheck.org/checklist-for-checklists.html.

_____

7. **Choose your response format, if required.** Some checklists require users to explicitly acknowledge that they have covered each checklist item. For example, a checklist used to certify that software meets a particular standard of consistency requires explicit responses, including signatures from the checklist administrator. In the development of a checklist, you may need to include a response format that allows for some flexibility. Following are examples of response formats for checklists:

   a. ☐ *Checkbox:* The user of the checklist explicitly indicates that an item on the checklist has been covered by filling in or clicking on the checkbox.

   b. *Yes/No:* This is useful when your checklist items are questions. An example of a portion of a checklist using the Yes/No format is shown below for items that might be used in a questionnaire quality checklist.

Use this checklist to evaluate the usability of each question on your questionnaire	Circle YES or NO for each question
Is the question a "double question"?	YES NO
Does the question have a technical term that won't be understood by respondents?	YES NO
Is the reference period missing (e.g., "during the last month")?	YES NO
Does the question require respondents to perform complex mental operations?	YES NO
Can the question be interpreted in multiple ways?	YES NO

   c. *Always, Most of the Time, Sometimes, Never.* A frequency response is appropriate, for example, if you are asking people how often they performed a task during a specified time period.

   d. *Tick marks (⊮⊮).* You might place tick marks on a checklist that you use to record activities during usability testing or observational studies. For example, an observer might make a tick mark when a person does something that generates an error message or uses particular features of a product. If you are using some form of tick mark, make sure that the form can handle extreme cases (you observed an unexpected but extremely high frequency behavior). For example, a user was once observed accessing a particular function on a graphics product several hundred times in an hour and the observer nearly used up every bit of white space on the front and back of a behavior checklist.

8. **Have colleagues familiar with the domain review the checklist.** General review questions include the following:
   a. Are the items in the checklist technically correct?
   b. Can the checklist be used effectively across the potential environments and contexts of use? For example, can you use the checklist in the rain or a darkened room?
   c. Are you missing any critical items?
   d. Are the items understandable?
   e. If you have conditional statements, is it clear to users where they should go next?
   f. Are the response categories appropriate? For example, you might need an N/A (not applicable) item or room to write in surprises.

9. **Revise the checklist, and conduct a usability evaluation on the checklist using it as realistically as possible.** One approach to testing a checklist is to have a sample of potential users think aloud as they apply the checklist to a realistic problem. You can also ask a sample of people to use the list and then conduct a survey or phone interview to get feedback on the checklist.

10. **Incorporate changes for the usability evaluation, and edit the checklist for technical and stylistic consistency.**

11. **Conduct a validation test to see if the checklist meets your original goals.** The criteria might be, for example:
    a. Does the checklist differentiate between "bad" and "good" (evaluation checklist)?
    b. Does the checklist capture most of the activities that are important for an observational study (behavior sampling checklist)?
    c. Does the checklist provide clear reminders about steps in a process such as a preflight (or in this case a prestudy) checklist?

12. **Revise the checklist based on the validation test.**

13. **Publish the checklist.** Provide a mechanism for distributing the checklist.

After Using the Checklist
After using the checklist, follow these steps:

1. **Gather feedback from your users on the usefulness and usability of the checklist.**
2. **Update the checklist based on feedback from users or changes to the target of the checklist.** If you had a usability defect checklist for graphical user interface (GUI) applications, you would update that checklist when you move from GUI applications to web or mobile applications.
3. **Provide a contact and mechanism to collect feedback from future users of the checklist.**

MAJOR ISSUES IN THE USE OF CHECKLISTS

There are some issues that often surface during the design and use of checklists. This section highlights some of these issues.

Checklist Philosophy
If you plan to develop a checklist, you might inquire, formally or informally, how others in your organization feel about checklists. "Checklist philosophy" is the organizational attitude toward the use of checklists. In some organizations, the use of checklists may be considered an important (or in the case of aircraft pilots, critical) aspect of the job performance; in other organizations, checklists may be regarded as busywork and possibly useful but not highly regarded or relied on. When considering the use of a checklist in a particular organization, consider its overall impact and how others might view the checklist weeks or months later. Will it be viewed as a useful tool that will have a positive impact on a product or process, or will it be perceived as an impediment to progress? Additional questions related to checklist philosophy include the following:

• Is your checklist required or mandatory?
• Who is the owner of the checklist? In many companies, the original creator or owner may have left long ago leaving responsibility for updates in a vacuum.

- Are there any rewards for appropriate use of checklists?
- What is the process for revising the checklist?
- How do you track checklist usage?
- How will you advertise the availability of checklists to new employees?
- How do you remind long-term employees to use the tool?

Checklist Heuristics

There are some general heuristics for creating checklists. Here is a list of checklist heuristics derived from Brykczynski (1999); Burian (2004, 2006); Gilb and Graham (1993), and others. These heuristics deal with text style and formatting, the demands of the usage scenarios for the checklist (will you be using this in a dynamic or stressful situation?), and overall checklist goals.

- **Design the physical form of the checklist so that it is usable for the range of anticipated situations.** Will you use the checklist outside, in windy environments, in bright sun, inside vehicles at night, and so on? A checklist needs to be usable across the range of expected settings.
- **Keep checklists short but not too short.** When you see a heuristic about the length of a particular artifact, keep in mind that the goal of the checklist can affect what "short" means. For example, this heuristic may not apply to checklists that are used to "certify" that a product meets a technical standard with hundreds of requirements. Additionally, a checklist that is too concise might not provide details to less-experienced users. As in questionnaire design, checklist length needs to be considered in context with understandability, clarity, and the motivation of the users.
- **Consider mental workload when you are designing your checklist.** You can have a very short checklist with a high mental workload and a long checklist with a low mental workload. The mental workload associated with your checklist depends on internal factors (readability, clarity of list items) and external factors (physical and environmental demands).
- **Ensure that the checklist items are not too general.** A checklist item that states "The home page is clean" may be too general. What does "clean" mean—a lack of clutter, the use of a small palette of colors, fields that line up...?

- **Avoid checklists that are too specific.** This heuristic is in a dynamic tension with the previous heuristic dealing with generality.
- **Ensure that all terminology, acronyms, and abbreviations will be understood by all potential users.** A common myth in work domains is that everyone knows the terminology. Does everyone know what "ASA" means, for example (Adaptive Security Algorithm, Adaptive Server Anywhere, Abaxial Spherical Aberration)? If you start asking your colleagues what acronyms or abbreviations mean, you are likely to discover that your ignorance is shared with many other slightly embarrassed colleagues.
- **Phrase items consistently in the form of questions or imperatives.** Checklists can be developed so that you ask a question and then provide Yes/No/Not Sure answers, or you can phrase items as imperative statements ("Verify that all icons have intelligible Alt + text.").
- **Provide an option indicating that the checklist item is "not applicable" or "not relevant."** In some situations, not all items will be relevant.
- **Follow a consistent style in the formatting and layout of the checklist items.**
- **Ensure that checklists are updated to reflect changes in supporting documents.** For example, if you create a checklist to determine conformance with a UI style guide, you must keep the checklist and style guide synchronized, which is not an easy task.
- **Consider whether your checklist should follow a DO-CONFIRM style (you complete a task and then ask for confirmation) or a READ-DO style (you read a checklist item, then complete that item, then note that you have completed it).**

How Do Checklist Evaluations Compare with Other Types of Evaluations?

Substantial amounts of literature compare heuristic evaluations with other types of usability evaluations, and this literature might be somewhat relevant; however, in much of that literature, it is not always clear how much people used checklists as the sole tool for uncovering problems. Thelin, Runeson, and Wohlin (2003) conducted a software inspection study, which compared a usage-based reading technique versus a checklist reading technique. Usage-based readings provide reviewers with use cases, user goals, and variations and exceptions to the use cases. In the checklist-based reading technique, reviewers use a list of issues that prompt them about what kinds of problems, defects, or faults to look for. Thelin et al. (2003) found that the usage-based reading technique was generally superior to the checklist technique. Evaluation checklists that are designed to support the finding of defects should be only one method of many that are used to assess the quality of a product. The use of multiple methods is called method triangulation.

Method Triangulation

Method triangulation involves the use of different research methods such as evaluation checklists, focus groups, usability testing, and event logging to understand the user experience. For example, if you wanted to find out what the most important problems were with the last version of a product, you could review old usability test reports, the results of heuristic evaluation checklist reviews, the corporate bug database, the minutes from customer feedback breakfasts, and data from a year-long customer panel. The use of several data-collection methods are more likely to indicate core problems (those problems that affect many user groups across customers) than any single method alone, as well as reveal more problems than any single method.

Required, Recommended, or Optional?

Some checklists are used to "certify" that a product follows standards and guidelines. For certification checklists, it is important to indicate whether a checklist item is Required, Recommended, or Optional, and then include Yes, No, Not Applicable (N/A) choices. Here is a simple example.

```
Context-Sensitive Help
Required [ ]yes [ ]no [ ]n/a
Your software provides context-sensitive help for
every feature. The user should never get a "help not
available" message.
Resizable Dialogs
Recommended [ ]yes [ ]no [ ]n/a
Dialogs that provide users with a list of file names
or object names should be resizable.
Save the User's Context
Required [ ]yes [ ]no [ ]n/a
```

Save the context for the user whenever possible. For example, if a user has positioned a dialog on the right side of a screen, then you should save the location for subsequent invocations of the same dialog.

DATA ANALYSIS

How do you analyze data from a checklist? The particular analysis will vary with the goals of the checklist and the type of checklist, and there could be hundreds of ways of analyzing checklist data. Here is a brief list of some general data analysis techniques.

Frequency Counts
Perhaps the most basic method for analyzing checklists involves counting the number of items for each response category (e.g., Yes/No) and reporting the frequencies for each response.

Comparison Against Criteria
In this technique, you compare the results of a checklist against a quantitative criterion. So, you might, for example, compare the percentage of Yes answers to a criterion value that 90% of the answers must have a Yes answer.

Frequency and Severity of Items
The data from many evaluation checklists (e.g., a heuristic evaluation checklist) can be represented by the frequency and severity technique. You first use the checklist as a guide to finding problems and then you rate the severity of each problem according to a severity scale (e.g., minor, moderate, major, catastrophic). Some organizations have criteria for how many problems are permitted; for example, no major or catastrophic problems are allowed. If a checklist is used to find problems or defects, then there are other potential measures of effectiveness (how many problems of different severities have been found relative to all problems), and efficiency, which might be the number of problems or defects found per unit of time.

Certification Criteria
Checklists that are the basis for official certification may require 100% agreement on required items (sometimes with the possibility of

exemptions from the certification organization). Checklists meant for less formal evaluation may use the percentage of agreement with items as a rough estimate of the quality of the product or process on a specified dimension.

Procedural Checklist

If a checklist is used to verify that a set of tasks has been performed (such as the steps in setting up a usability laboratory for a test session or the steps that pilots go through before landing), the data might be considered binary; that is, either all the steps have been followed (pass) or not (fail).

Checklist Effectiveness

The final technique is measuring the effectiveness of checklists. In this data analysis technique, there are several issues to consider, including the agreement among different reviewers of the same product, their understanding of the checklist items, and whether the checklist was actually used by reviewers.

RECOMMENDED READINGS

Brykczynski, B. (1999). A survey of software inspection checklists. *SIGSOFT Software Engineering Notes, 24*(1), 82.

Drury, C. G. (2012). Human factors and ergonomics audits. In Gavriel Salvendy (Ed.), *Handbook of human factors and ergonomics* (4th ed.). Hoboken, NJ: Wiley.

Gawande, A. (2009). *The checklist manifesto: How to get things right.* New York, NY: Metropolitan Books.

Stanton, N. A., Salmon, P. M., Walker, G. H., Baber, C., & Jenkins, D. P. (2005). *Human factors methods: A practical guide for engineering and design.* Aldershot, Hampshire: Ashgate Publishing Company.

REFERENCES

Baker, K., Greenberg, S., & Gutwin, C. (2002). *Empirical development of a heuristic evaluation methodology for shared workspace groupware* (pp. 96–105). In: *Proceedings of the 2002 ACM conference on computer supported cooperative work* (CSCW '02). New York, NY: ACM.

Bevan, N., & Macleod, M. (1994). Usability measurement in context. *Behavior and Information Technology, 13*, 132–145.

Brykczynski, B. (1999). A survey of software inspection checklists. *SIGSOFT Software Engineering Notes, 24*(1), 82.

Burian, B. K. (2004). *Emergency and abnormal checklist design factors influencing flight crew response: A case study.* In: *Proceedings of the international conference on human–computer interaction in aeronautics* 2004. Toulouse, France: EURISCO International.

Burian, B.K. (2006). Design guidance for emergency and abnormal checklists in aviation. In: *The proceedings of the human factors and ergonomics society 50th annual meeting*. San Francisco.

Edgerton, E. A., Draper, S. W., & Barton, S. B. (1993). Feature checklists in HCI: Some basic results. In S. Ashlund, K. Mullet, A. Henderson, E. Hollnagel, & T. White (Eds.), *INTERACT '93 and CHI '93 conference companion on human factors in computing systems* (pp. 189−190). New York, NY: ACM PressAmsterdam, The Netherlands, April 24−29, 1993.

Gilb, T., & Graham, D. (1993). *Software inspection*. Reading, MA: Addison-Wesley.

Henry, S. L. (2007). *Just ask: Integrating accessibility throughout design*. Madison, WI: ET\Lawton.

Kaptelinin, V., Nardi, B. A., & Macaulay, C. (1999). Methods and tools: The activity checklist: a tool for representing the "space" of context. *Interactions, 6*, 4.

Lee, K. I., Jin, B. S., & Ji, Y. G. (2011). The scenario-based usability checklist development for home appliance design: A case study. *Human Factors and Ergonomics in Manufacturing and Service Industries, 21*, 1.

Martin, B., & Hanington, B. (2012). *Universal methods of design: 100 ways to research complex problems, develop innovative ideas, and design effective solutions*. Beverly, MA: Rockport Publishers.

Nielsen, J., & Molich, R. (1990). Heuristic evaluation of user interfaces. In J. Carrasco Chew, & J. Whiteside (Eds.), *Proceedings of the SIGCHI conference on human factors in computing systems* (CHI '90) (pp. 249−256). New York, NY: ACM Press.

Pierotti, D. (n.d.). *Heuristic evaluation: A system checklist*. Retrieved May 30, 2013 from <http://www.stcsig.org/usability/topics/articles/he-checklist.html>.

Quinn, S.D., Souppaya, M.P., Cook, M., & Scarfone, K.A. (2011). *SP 800−70 Rev. 2. National checklist program for its products: Guidelines for checklist users and developers*. Technical Report. Gaithersburg, MD: NIST.

Thelin, T., Runeson, P., & Wohlin, C. (2003). An experimental comparison of usage-based and checklist-based reading. *IEEE Transactions on Software Engineering, 29*(8), 687−704.

Wieringa, R., Condori-Fernandez, N., Daneva, M., Mutschler, B., & Pastor, O. (2012). *Lessons learned from evaluating a checklist for reporting experimental and observational research* ((pp. 157−160)). In: *Proceedings of the ACM-IEEE international symposium on empirical software engineering and measurement (ESEM '12*. New York, NY: ACM Press.

Wilson, C. (2009). *The consistency conundrum*. Retrieved June 2, 2013 from <http://dux.typepad.com/dux/2009/03/the-consistency-conundrum.html>.

Questionnaires and Surveys

The important thing is not to stop questioning. Curiosity has its own reason for existing.

—Albert Einstein

Alternate Names: Polls, questionnaire study

Related Methods: Critical incident technique, diary method, phone interview, semi-structured interview, structured interview

OVERVIEW OF QUESTIONNAIRES AND SURVEYS

A questionnaire is a written, online, or verbal tool for collecting data from individuals or groups that can be analyzed using qualitative and quantitative techniques. Building on the concepts introduced in Chapter 1, this chapter serves as a checklist on how to develop questions, questionnaires, and surveys. Developing a questionnaire is only one aspect of a survey. Other aspects of survey design include the following:

- *Devising a sampling plan*: Who are the respondents and how many respondents do you need to provide reliable and valid results? If you have a bad sample, your data might lead the product team astray.
- *Developing a data analysis plan*: What types of data will help you meet your goals? What analyses will help you understand the raw data?
- *Recruiting respondents*: Recruiting the target respondents is often a struggle, especially with privacy, opt-out policies, anti-spam policies, and difficulties getting directly at users (as opposed to customers).

- *Writing cover letters and introductions that explain your study*: Good cover letters can influence response rates.
- *Sending out follow-up reminders*: Reminders can be quite effective at encouraging responses, but they need to be written to be both gentle and persuasive so the respondent is not irritated.
- *Analyzing the data*: For large-scale studies, it is useful to consult with a business analyst or statistician who can guide you through data analysis issues such as inflated alpha levels (when you do multiple statistical tests on the same set of data, you are more likely to find spurious significant results) and confidence intervals (a way to assess the uncertainty due to sampling around statistics, such as means).
- *Interpreting the data*: What do your data mean? Interpretation involves both art and science. You need to understand how the sampling and context of your study can affect your results.
- *Presenting the data to stakeholders*: What is the best approach for presenting your data? How much do you present? How much detail do you need to ensure credibility?

This chapter focuses on the fundamentals of questionnaire design, practical tips, and some selected topics related to the broader survey process. A large collection of research on how to design, conduct, and analyze surveys (Bradburn, Sudman, & Wansink, 2004; Converse & Presser, 1986; Dillman, Smyth, & Christian, 2009; Foddy, 1993; Groves et al., 2009) is available, but the research can be confusing, contradictory, and complex. The intent of this chapter is to provide some reasonable practical advice, based on many years of reviewing and improving questionnaires, and not to debate in depth whether a five-point scale is necessarily better or worse than a seven-point scale.

●●●————————————————————————————————

The Long History of Surveys and Questionnaires

One of the earliest surveys on record is described in the *Domesday Book*, which reported on a land survey commissioned in 1085 by William the Conqueror to determine who owned land and other resources in England. The survey results were used to determine how much tax could be extracted from the landowners.

Around 800 years later, in the 1870s, Sir Francis Galton, the Victorian polymath and cousin of Charles Darwin, introduced the modern questionnaire method into psychology with his controversial book,

English Men of Science: Their Nature and Nurture (Galton, 1874). Galton used the questionnaire method to examine whether interest in science was due to heredity or environment by sending questionnaires to 190 members of the Royal Society and asking questions about environment, birth order, and characteristics of the parents of Society members.

A questionnaire is often viewed as an easy way to gather data quickly from many respondents. However, the common belief that questionnaires are easy to design (often expressed as "let us just throw a questionnaire together" by those with limited questionnaire design experience) is a myth. The design of questionnaires and surveys is a complex process that involves many, sometimes conflicting, considerations (Dillman, 2000, 2007; Dillman et al., 2009; Kirakowski, 2000; Nemeth, 2004; Robson, 2002; Sudman, Bradburn, & Schwarz 1996), including some basic assumptions:

- The questionnaire is tapping the concepts of interest.
- The potential respondents are competent sources of the information you need.
- The respondents are willing to commit the time to answer your questionnaire (this gets into relevance and extrinsic and intrinsic motivation).
- All of the respondents understand your questions in the same way.
- People will follow the rules of the survey and provide (to the best of their abilities) honest data.

This chapter describes the basic procedures for developing paper and online questionnaires and highlights some of the important considerations for designing questionnaires and conducting surveys, including the following:

- *The structure of questions*: When should you use open, closed, or mixed questions? Mixed questions include both specific responses and an open-ended "Other" response that allows respondents to write in an answer not provided.
- *The wording of questions and responses*: Changing a single word, even one that seems innocuous, could change the pattern of responses.
- *Question order*: Each question you ask can influence the answers to subsequent questions. In the extreme, asking something that is too

threatening or personal at the beginning of a questionnaire might result in the respondent rejecting your survey immediately. Deciding how to order questions is, like other aspects of questionnaire design, part art and part science.

- *Biases*: Bias can be subtle or blatant and show up in the design of questionnaire layouts, instructions, questions, and responses. Here are a few examples of biases that can creep in questionnaire and survey design. Others will be discussed throughout this chapter.
  - *Primacy/recency*: The tendency to choose the first or last responses in an unordered list. In online or mailed questionnaires, respondents may tend to choose one of the first few responses. If the respondents are being asked questions in a telephone survey, there may be a bias to answer by choosing the most recent choice.
  - *End aversion or central tendency bias*: The tendency to avoid extreme choices such as "Extremely Disagree" or "Extremely Agree."
  - *Leading questions*: The tendency to answer in the direction suggested by questions like "Don't you agree that ....?"
- *Sampling*: Many types of sampling are available, and questionnaire designers should be aware of the strengths and weaknesses of their particular sampling approach. This is covered in more detailed later in this chapter.

WHEN SHOULD YOU USE QUESTIONNAIRES AND SURVEYS?

Questionnaires and surveys can be used throughout the development process (Table 2.1), from problem definition to implementation and maintenance.

Table 2.2 illustrates the relative effort required, on average, to develop and use questionnaires and surveys. As this chapter highlights in multiple places, questionnaire and survey design requires broad

Table 2.1 Phases of Development When Questionnaires Are Useful				
✓	✓	✓	✓	✓
Problem Definition	Requirements	Conceptual Design	Detailed Design	Implementation

Table 2.2 Relative Effort and Resources Required for Checklist Development and Use				
Overall Effort Required	Time for Planning and Conducting	Skill and Experience	Supplies and Equipment	Time for Data Analysis and Interpretation
▨▨▨☐☐	▨▨▨▨☐	▨▨▨☐☐	▨▨☐☐☐	▨▨▨▨

knowledge and attention to detail, so the effort to develop questionnaires and surveys can range from moderate to high.

Questionnaires and surveys can be used in product design to:

- Serve as checklists. As noted in Chapter 1, many checklists are in the form of a questionnaire, and many of the principles for creating good checklists and questionnaires are the same.
- Provide the foundation for face-to-face interviews, online data collection, and phone interviews.
- Collect subjective measures on attributes such as satisfaction, comfort, and aesthetics.
- Collect information about respondents to describe who is using a product or to screen people for inclusion in UCD activities.
- Gather information about behaviors (e.g., "How often do you use Product X?").
- Compare reactions to different products or reactions to the same product over time.
- Gather data from distant respondents when other methods are too costly.
- Complement other methods by adding breadth to your data. For example, you might be able to interview a dozen users across several cities and then use what you learned from those interviews to craft a questionnaire that expands the breadth of your research.

As is the case with checklists, questionnaires have both strengths and weaknesses that you should consider.

Strengths
Questionnaires have the following strengths:

- They can be administered to large numbers of people using a variety of methods, such as e-mail, online survey tools, regular mail, face-to-face interviews, or phone interviews.

- The use of questionnaires is more anonymous than face-to-face interviews.
- Standardized questionnaires allow you to compare responses across various groups and products.
- Results can be used as input to other methods such as interviews, focus groups, and usability testing.
- Modern online tools make basic data analysis easy and fast (though interpretation still requires the human touch).

Weaknesses

Questionnaires have the following weaknesses:

- Many user-centered design (UCD) practitioners have little formal training in questionnaire and survey design issues, and their questionnaires can suffer from this lack of training.
- Questionnaire design requires a wide range of knowledge and training. To develop high-quality questionnaires and surveys, you need some grounding in sampling methods, questionnaire construction, qualitative and quantitative data analysis, cognitive biases that influence responses, and data interpretation approaches.
- Questionnaires, like other self-report methods, suffer from problems of recall, order effects, context effects, and estimation bias.
- Questionnaires with many open-ended questions can generate large amounts of data that take significant effort to analyze and more time to interpret.
- Return rates can be low with online and mail surveys, and the nature of the sample is not always clear.
- Online and mail questionnaires are not as flexible as interviews or focus groups where you can ask follow-up questions.
- Survey fatigue, the overuse of online surveys, can be a serious problem, even for normally dedicated respondents. The ease with which you can create an online survey and the expansion of "data-driven" product groups can result in potential respondents thinking "Not another questionnaire—I'm so tired of filling out these questionnaires!"
- Privacy laws have become a barrier to online and mailed surveys.

WHAT DO YOU NEED TO USE QUESTIONNAIRES AND SURVEYS?

This section provides a brief description of the logistical aspects of questionnaire and survey design.

Personnel, Participants, and Training

Good questionnaire design requires training in the process and principles of questionnaire design and survey implementation. Many good books are available on questionnaire design that can aid practitioners. Serious efforts to build a reliable and valid measurement tool for comparing products against each other or established norms requires a significant development effort and the assistance of a statistician or psychometrician.

Software

Online software tools come in a wide variety. Some can be used free for small surveys but require additional payment for large studies. Table 2.3 shows examples of online questionnaire and survey software available in 2013.

Before choosing online survey software, you should verify that it provides the design features you need and is usable for both the creator and the respondent. These features and usability attributes include the following:

- The types of questions and response categories you need
- Appropriate navigation
- Accessibility features (e.g., does it work well with screen readers)
- Screening features
- Branching as a result of filter questions
- Password protection
- Progress indicators to show people how much they have done and how much more to do
- The ability to change earlier questions (you may not want this if you are using screening or filter questions)
- Suitable data formats for exporting the results to Excel®, IBM®, SPSS®, or another analysis program)

Table 2.3 Examples of Online Survey Software	
Product Name	**URL**
Zoomerang	http://www.zoomerang.com
SurveyGizmo	http://www.surveygizmo.com
Qualtrics	http://www.qualtrics.com
SurveyMonkey	http://www.surveymonkey.com
Listen-Up	http://www.constantcontact.com

- Data analysis capabilities and flexibility of analyses (some free systems may not provide all the detail you need in your analysis)
- Error checking as questions are answered
- Drop-out rates (how many people quit your survey before the end)
- Level of usability appropriate for your target respondents

Documents and Materials
The documents and materials necessary for designing questionnaires and surveys include the following:

- Survey project plan
- Data collection plan
- Recruiting screeners (the prestudy questionnaire used to select appropriate respondents)
- Survey forms
- Cover letters
- Thank you notes

PROCEDURES AND PRACTICAL ADVICE

This section describes how to create useful and usable questionnaires and surveys. Solid planning provides a foundation for a successful survey so this section starts with some detailed procedures and best practices for planning your survey. Then there are some best practices for conducting your study. And last, there is a discussion about what to do after you have your data. Tips and tricks that this author has learned from working on hundreds of surveys are sprinkled liberally throughout this section.

Planning and Developing the Questionnaire and Survey
Design a questionnaire like you would design a product (except that your design cycle might be measured in days or weeks rather than months or years). Start by gathering requirements from your stakeholders. What do your stakeholders need to know about users, their tasks, environments, and the product? Define your goals for the questionnaire. Describe explicitly how to build trust and provide respondents with benefits that outweigh the costs of filling out the questionnaire. Create a prototype questionnaire, and go through several rounds of iterative evaluation. Finally, make sure that you have a data analysis plan so you know what to do with the data.

Consider both quantitative metrics of quality—coverage error, sampling error, nonresponse bias—and qualitative measures of quality—relevance, credibility, and timeliness (Groves et al., 2009).

You can follow this general procedure for planning and developing a questionnaire and adapt it to the specific goals of your project:

1. **Determine the purpose of your data collection.** The first, and most important question you need to ask is, "What is the purpose of my data collection?" People who are not experts in questionnaire design often make the mistake of having a vague idea about collecting data and then decide to send out a questionnaire because it is considered quick and easy to create and distribute. They have no clear purpose for the data collection other than, "We need some data!" Start your questionnaire study by clarifying the purpose of your data collection. A questionnaire can have a number of purposes, including the following:
   a. Understanding user needs
   b. Gathering information about particular attributes of your users, their tasks, and environments
   c. Validating design decisions
   d. Understanding user attitudes or opinions
   e. Comparing the attitudes of different groups
   f. Gathering facts
   g. Assessing product usability or satisfaction
   h. Gathering information comparing competitive products
   i. Eliciting knowledge from experts
   j. Convincing management to do something different

   Too often, the purpose of each question on the questionnaire is not clear. Each question should relate to a specific business goal and user experience goal, or hypothesis. You might consider creating a matrix as shown in the example in Table 2.4, where you make these connections explicit.
   If there is not a clear business or user experience goal for a particular question, eliminate that question. Avoid the temptation to piggyback random questions or questions from other groups to your questionnaire. If you are forced to piggyback for political reasons, do what you can to ensure that at least the questions are well formulated.

Table 2.4 Connecting Questions with Business and User Experience Goals		
Business Goal	**User Experience Goal**	**Type of Question**
Get new people on our system	High learnability	• Rating scale question about ease of learning • Open-ended or closed question that asks about initial learning problems
Reduce drop-outs during ordering process	More usable shopping cart	• Question about difficulties with the shopping cart

2. **Decide if a questionnaire study is the appropriate method for collecting data to answer your business and user experience questions.** If you are planning to use a questionnaire, consider whether it is the appropriate method for gathering the data you need to answer design, process, or business questions:

   a. Can questionnaire data provide useful information that will answer your design or business questions? If you want detailed task information, for example, a questionnaire is probably not appropriate (although it could be a starting point). Getting at task details might require an observational study, a hierarchical task analysis, or an experience mapping session with a group of users.

   b. Do you have enough information on the topic to design a useful questionnaire? You might need to conduct some phone interviews or face-to-face interviews, or review existing data to understand the critical issues before you create a questionnaire.

   c. Do the benefits of designing a questionnaire and survey outweigh the costs involved?

   d. Do you have the resources necessary to design and implement a questionnaire study? Many inexpensive tools are available (e.g., SurveyMonkey), but making sense of large amounts of qualitative data from open-ended questions can be very time consuming.

   e. Can you gather valid and reliable data using a questionnaire? It is important to be aware of the biases inherent in your questionnaire and survey design. Consider how you will choose the sample of users for your survey. Are you sampling only your "best and favorite" customers, a random sample of customers, or have you included a broad range of customers? Your best and favorite customer may not want to be too negative and may give socially desirable answers that lead you to create flawed designs.

    f. Do you have access to a reasonable sample of respondents who match your target audience?

3. **Gather requirements and general questions from stakeholders.** Many techniques are available for gathering requirements for questionnaires. Here are a few suggestions:

    a. *Interview* key stakeholders about what they know and do not know about users and how they use a product. Stakeholders include actual users, and personnel in sales, marketing, development, documentation, training, senior management, and technical support.

    b. *Brainstorm* with the product team about what they want to learn from a questionnaire study. If you can do this as part of a regular product team meeting, you can get many of the stakeholders in the room at the same time. This author's book, *Brainstorming and Beyond: A User-Centered Design Method* (Wilson, 2013), provides many tips for effective face-to-face brainstorming and related ideation methods.

    c. *Distribute 3 × 5 cards at meetings or individually,* and ask stakeholders from different groups to write one to three questions that they would like to ask users. Avoid asking for too much here. This technique can be useful for getting insight into what issues are most important for different groups.

    d. *Conduct a short brainwriting session.* Brainwriting (Wilson, 2013) is a variation on brainstorming where each person writes a question on a card and then passes it on to the next person who then reads the previous question, adds a new question, and passes the card on to the next person who sees the first two questions and adds a third question. The premise here is that seeing the questions of others will prompt additional relevant questions. This can be done in about 10 to 15 minutes at team meetings and yields a large selection of questions quickly.

Weblink

For more on brainwriting, go to http://dux.typepad.com and enter "brainwriting Chauncey" into the search field. This will take you to a short article on the brainwriting method.

e. *Conduct a focus group* to find out what issues are important to key stakeholders and target user groups. Focus groups can be a good source of requirements for questionnaire design because they tend to bring out spontaneous reactions, unexpected questions, preferences, and organizational issues that may not emerge from other data collection methods (Krueger & Casey, 2000; Kuniavsky, 2003; Langford & McDonagh, 2003). The more open-ended nature of a focus group is ideal for providing input for more structured online or paper questionnaires.

4. **Consider whether you have enough experience and training to design, implement, and analyze the data from a questionnaire study.** The design of questionnaires requires background experience in many areas, such as scale development, psychometrics (theories and methods of psychological measurement), sampling, and content analysis. If your training is limited, and the results are going to have a significant impact on your product, consider hiring a consultant or finding colleagues who can help with design, sampling, analysis, and other implementation issues. You might look to the marketing organization for colleagues with questionnaire and survey design experience.

5. **Determine the sampling requirements for your questionnaire study.** Sampling is a complex topic that generally involves the following three basic steps:

   a. *Specify or at least acknowledge the sampling process.* Here are some of the most common sampling methods (McBurney, 1998):

      • *Probability samples*, where respondents are chosen in a way that is representative of the population. Probability samples are amenable to statistical inference but are extremely hard to obtain in practice because there is often no easy way to get access to everyone in a population. The two major types of probability samples are random (each person in a population has the same probability of being chosen) and stratified (you sample proportionately from the different subgroups in a population).

      • *Haphazard samples*, where "hit-or-miss" methods are used to select respondents. The prototypical haphazard sample might be the "person on the street" interviews done by local television stations or graduate students where people are stopped on the street and asked to respond to particular questions, such as "Do you ever download free music?" or "How do you use search engines at home?"

- *Convenience samples*, where respondents are chosen for practical reasons such as proximity, cost, and access. Convenience samples are common in UCD and can be useful for developing hypotheses early in a project, understanding the background of users and other stakeholders, and defining response alternatives for subsequent questionnaires.
- *Purposive samples*, where the respondents are chosen for a specific purpose. For example, you might want to interview professors teaching classes in human—computer interaction (HCI) at the top 25 universities about their curriculum rather than a random sample of all the universities where HCI is taught.
- *Snowball sampling*, where a small group of initial candidates nominate people through friendships, business relationships, and social networks. This nonprobability method is useful when you are looking for experts in areas where no clear list is available from which to recruit. Snowball sampling is very dependent on the initial participants who are asked to recruit others with a particular background.

It is important to acknowledge the limitations of these sampling methods and include that information in any reports that are generated. For detailed information on sampling theory, different sampling methods, and specific sampling procedures, see Lohr (1999) and Levy and Lemeshow (1999). Kuniavsky (2003, pp. 328—335) has an excellent and understandable discussion of sampling and potential biases.

b. *Compile a list of people in the target populations from which you can choose a sample, or decide how and where you are going to publicize the survey to recruit your respondents.* For example, if you were interested in surveying usability colleagues on what methods they use most in their work, you might post notices on usability discussion groups, send e-mails to people you know, and hand out cards at regional or international conferences with instructions on how to find and fill out the survey. Your recruiting message can contain a link to a screening questionnaire if you are conducting a purposive sample where you want respondents with a particular mix of skills, experience, and traits.

c. *Select the sample.* Select your sample based on your business and experience goals and sampling method. Keep in mind that the response rate to a survey request can have a wide range depending on incentives, motivation, importance to the respondent, and "survey fatigue." This author has personally experienced response rates ranging from a few percent to over 50%.

6. **What general questions should I ask?** After you select the types of information that fit the purposes of the study, you need to translate those ideas into general questions without yet worrying about detailed formatting or response categories. The process of going from ideas or topics to general questions is challenging. You first need to be clear on what type of information you are looking for: knowledge, behavior, attitudes or some mix of these. Then you must consider what question structure and wording best fits your target respondents. As you develop some general ideas about your questions, think about how to give your question structure and wording the following characteristics:
   a. Motivating to the respondent
   b. Interpretable by multiple respondents in the same way
   c. Answerable accurately (e.g., whether respondents can recall and report on past behaviors)
   d. Relevant to all respondents
   The next steps in the process provide some guidelines on how to design individual questions.

7. **What type of question structure should I use?** After you decide on what information you want to collect, you need to decide what type of question to ask. There are two general types of questions: open-ended and closed-ended. Open-ended questions permit respondents to answer in their own words, whereas closed-ended questions impose a set of response alternatives chosen by the questionnaire designers. Closed-ended (hereafter referred to as "closed") questions can be subdivided into questions with unordered response categories (e.g., a list of occupations) or ordered response categories (e.g., rating scales) (Dillman, 2000). Examples of open and closed structures are shown next.

Open question:
List two things that could be done to improve the DSL installation process.

Closed question with unordered choices:
Which one of these documents is most useful to you? (Check one answer.)
_____ User's Guide

___ Getting Started Manual
___ Reference Manual
___ Quick Lookup Card

Closed question with ordered choices:

How often do you use [Product Name Goes Here] in a typical week? (Check one answer.)

___ I don't use the product at all
___ 1−2 times a week
___ 3−5 times a week
___ 6−10 times a week
___ More than 10 times a week

●●●───

Mutually Exclusive Responses

When you have ordered choices, make sure that the choices do not overlap. Your answers should be mutually exclusive. For example, consider the following choices:

__1−3 times a week
__3−5 times a week
__ 5−7 times a week
__ 7−10 times a week

In this example, your response categories overlap and a respondent who did something once every workday (5 times a week) could choose either 3−5 times a week or 5−7 times a week. Make sure that your answers are mutually exclusive as in this example:

__ 1−2 times a week
__ 3−5 times a week
__ 6−8 times a week
__ 9−11 times a week

───

Advantages and disadvantages of each type of question structure are shown in Table 2.5 (Dillman, 2000, 2007; Nemeth, 2004; Salant & Dillman, 1994; Tullis & Albert, 2008).

8. **Evaluate your draft questions.** You can do this in several ways:
   a. Conduct an expert review where subject matter experts and experts in questionnaire design determine whether the questions are technically correct and follow questionnaire design guidelines.
   b. Ask a small focus group to review the questions for clarity, appropriate terminology, and scope.

Table 2.5 Advantages and Disadvantages of Open Questions Versus Closed Questions		
Question Structure	Advantages	Disadvantages
Open ended	• Useful when you do not know much about a particular topic and thus cannot generate credible response categories. • Useful when the list of known responses is very long. • Good for exploratory studies at the beginning of projects. • Helpful as a follow-up to a closed question. For example, if you ask a person to rate the usability of a system, you might want to ask respondents to explain their answers. • Useful for getting at strong opinions or topics that may have been missed by the questionnaire designer. • Efficient when you are asking questions that can be easily recalled without a list (e.g., "What state do you live in?").	• Can be demanding for respondents, especially if you ask too broad a question. • Typically produces many responses but only a few on each topic. • Takes significant coding effort. • Is sometimes difficult to compare the results of open-ended questions across the sample. Some participants may give very brief and cryptic answers while others provide detailed step-by-step explanations. • Higher nonresponse rate than closed questions. • Requires more time to answer.
Close-ended	• Easier for respondents to answer than open questions. • Easy to code and analyze. • Appropriate when you are certain that you have covered the list of possible responses.	• Respondents may feel that they have to choose an alternative that isn't what they view as the "best" answer. • Some closed questions require research to identify the appropriate response categories.

   c. Conduct brief interviews of potential respondents as they try to answer the questions and see if the questions and responses make sense.

9. **Create a prototype of the complete questionnaire, and review it against principles of questionnaire design.** Design a prototype questionnaire, including the cover page or, if online, the introductory screen, and review the prototype against principles of questionnaire design (in effect, conduct a questionnaire inspection using questionnaire and question design guidelines from this chapter and other references). These principles should cover questionnaire wording, relevance, page layout, response categories, consistency, and order. Interview a few people not closely associated with the project as they read the questionnaire and think aloud about their reactions to it. If you have survey experts, ask them to review the prototype for some of the subtle issues such as question order and rating scale appropriateness.

●●●─────────────────────────────────

Designing for Reuse

Some surveys may be reused by different people at different times. For example, a major customer satisfaction survey might be mined for open-ended content for several years by different groups of people. When designing a questionnaire and planning a survey, provide documentation (e.g., the coding scheme for open-ended data; the meaning of values in a spreadsheet [0 = No; 1 = Yes; 999 = No answer]) and any rules that emerged about how to handle odd data (e.g., a person notes in an open-ended question that he gave an "arbitrary" answer to an earlier question) that would help future reuse.

─────────────────────────────────

10. **Review the questions for relevance.** At this point in the planning of a questionnaire, you might do a final review of the relevance of each question to your business goals, design questions, or hypotheses. Relevance is an important attribute of questionnaires. Sometimes a tendency emerges to piggyback questions onto a proposed survey because the cost to the product team is minimal. However, the addition of marginal questions increases the possibility that respondents will view the questionnaire as too long or a waste of time. Bailey (1994) suggests that a survey designer assess relevance by briefly describing how each item in a questionnaire will be presented in the final report from the survey results.

11. **Consider how to establish trust, increase rewards, and reduce costs for respondents.** You can design your questionnaire to create trust among respondents and influence their expectations about the benefits and costs associated with filling out the questionnaire. Dillman (1978, 2000), approached questionnaire and survey design from the perspective of social exchange—a social psychological framework based on the theory that individual actions (such as filling out a questionnaire) are motivated by the return that those actions will bring to the respondent (e.g., better products, better service, more useful features in future products). To the extent that respondents feel that the costs of a survey are low, the rewards high, and the source trustworthy, the likelihood that they fill out and return a questionnaire increases. Dillman bases his approach to questionnaire and survey design on a large body of work on social exchange by Homans (1958), Blau (1964), Thibaut and Kelley (1959), and the work on persuasion by Cialdini (2001).

Table 2.6 Checklists of Ways to Increase Response Rates to a Survey
Reward, Cost, and Trust

Increase Rewards for the Respondent
- ☐ The questions are interesting to the respondents.
- ☐ The language in the survey is positive and makes the respondent feel like a collaborator.
- ☐ There is some tangible reward for filling out and submitting the survey.
- ☐ The respondent has been thanked.
- ☐ Questions are written to respect the respondent.

Decrease the Costs for the Respondent
- ☐ The questions are all relevant.
- ☐ The questionnaire is usable in paper, online, or verbal format.
- ☐ Respondents can change answers easily.
- ☐ The survey includes only important questions that relate to business and user experience goals (no piggybacked questions).
- ☐ Sensitive questions are phrased in a way that does not upset the respondent.

Increase the Respondent's Trust
- ☐ There is a clear statement about privacy.
- ☐ There is a clear statement about how the data will be used.
- ☐ The sponsor of the survey is explicit.
- ☐ The survey is signed by a senior person to improve respondent trust.
- ☐ There is a way to contact the sponsor of the survey for questions or to verify the legitimacy of the survey.

Table 2.6 is a checklist that you can use to assess whether respondents will be motivated to fill out and return your survey.

12. **Devise an explicit data analysis plan.** A useful but often neglected part of questionnaire design is the explicit description of the data analysis plan. A detailed data analysis plan should describe the following:

a. *How answers will be coded.* It is important to consider some of the common data coding issues that come up in different types of surveys:

- *Whether you need specific answer categories.* Examples include "Don't know," "No opinion," "Not applicable (N/A)," or "Refuse to answer."

- *How you will code missing data.* You might indicate missing data with a code that is clearly distinct from other answer codes (e.g., 999). If you are missing answers from a set of rating scales, for example, there are some techniques you can use for handling missing values (Allison, 2001), such as only using respondents who have no missing data on the variables of interest, or substituting the calculated mean of the variable for the completed cases into the missing values for the variable. Keep in mind that biases are implicit in each technique for handling missing data, and some help from a trained statistician is recommended.

- *How you will code unusual answers.* If a person circles two numbers on a rating scale on a paper questionnaire to assess posttest reactions, how will you code the answer? You might take the average of the two scores and use that in your data analysis, or you might choose the more conservative answer consistently. Key guidelines for coding unusual answers are to have a rule, to make that rule explicit, and then to apply it consistently for all similar responses. In your report, you can note the rules that you used when you had to deal with unusual data.
- *What method you will use for coding open-ended data.* For example, you could break the text for each open-ended question into "thought segments" and then use a set of predefined tags to categorize the text data, or you could take the segments and organize them into larger themes with an affinity diagram.
- *What analyses you will do on single questions and sets of questions.* Consider the following types of analyses:
  - Content analysis, the process of classifying a large set of words into fewer content categories.
  - Measures of central tendency (mean, median, mode) and variability (standard deviation, variance).
  - Outlier analysis (outliers are observations or results that deviate substantially from the rest of the sample and can represent measurement errors, biases, or the inadvertent mixing of two populations of respondents).
  - Exploratory analyses (box and whisker plots, histograms).
  - Confidence intervals.
- *Any hypotheses that you may have and what questions will be used to test those hypotheses.* You should do this even if you have survey software that does an automatic analysis of the data. You might find that your automated software does not allow some of the analyses you need to answer questions that are important to the goals of your questionnaire study.
- *Whether you want to cross-tabulate data from different questions.* For example, you might need software that allows cross tabulations (sometimes called pivot tables) that show how the data from two or more questions are associated.

For example, you might want to look at reactions to a product based on job title or years of experience in a field to see if any interactions or patterns occur in the data; for example, more experienced users rate their satisfaction with a product higher than less-experienced users. Cross tabulation shows how two questions are interrelated. If you are using Microsoft Excel, you can use the PivotTable function to create cross tabulations.

Weblink

You can find some good examples of cross tabulation at http://www.custominsight.com/articles/crosstab-sample.asp.

---

13. **Pilot test the questionnaire and tools you will use to present the questionnaire to respondents.** Pretesting questionnaires is essential for discovering flaws and usability issues with cover letters, the questionnaire itself, and the method of administration (e.g., paper or online). The best way to pretest is to have people who are potential respondents think aloud as they complete a questionnaire—a variation on think-aloud usability testing called the "user (or usability) edit" (Atlas, 1981, 1998; Meister, 1985; Soderston, 1985). Respondents should be encouraged to comment on any aspect of the questionnaire, including unclear or ambiguous questions, the completeness and clarity of the response categories, biased questions, terminology, legibility (Is the text size large enough for older respondents?), sentence structure, and threatening questions. If you are using an online questionnaire, the process also focuses on the navigation and error correction features of the online survey tool.

After a small sample of face-to-face interviews, do a full-blown pilot test using the particular survey method you have chosen (mail, online, face-to-face). Get a small sample of users (or people as close to the expected users as possible) and have them fill out the questionnaire under realistic conditions and give you feedback. Make your final changes based on this input and perform a final edit. If you are using a remote survey tool, you should do several remote pilot sessions to ensure that there are no problems with the online tools and that your specific survey tool works well with different browsers.

In your pretesting, you might aim for some diversity to ensure that the questionnaire design is clear for the entire range of your expected respondents (young versus old; inexperienced versus experienced).

Conducting the Questionnaire Study

After you have completed the previous steps, you are ready to implement your survey. Dillman et al. (2009) note that a well-constructed questionnaire is a good starting point, but many survey implementation details will have even more impact on response rates than the questionnaire you so carefully crafted and tested. Here are some of the more important implementation issues for paper and online surveys:

1. **Consider the best time to administer a questionnaire.** If you are planning to distribute paper questionnaires to a group, avoid handing out the surveys at the end of the day or shift. A better time to ask people to fill out a paper questionnaire (e.g., at a conference) is at a mid-morning or afternoon break. If you are using questionnaires as part of a field study, consider arranging time during the workday so respondents can complete the questionnaire as part of their normal work (this might make it seem more rewarding and relevant) (Charlton, 2002). Avoid distributing surveys during peak periods for your respondents such as the end of the business year, the end of a quarter in the United States, or during a critical project. Examine your calendar for national and international secular and religious holidays that might coincide with your proposed questionnaire distribution dates.

2. **Develop a plan for follow-up for those who don't respond midway through your survey open dates.** The degree of follow-up will depend on your relationships with respondents. You might be sending questionnaires to carefully selected good customers, so your follow-up may be a single personal e-mail. In contrast to a simple e-mail reminder, Dillman (2000, p. 151) suggests a five-phase "contact" plan for mailed questionnaires that can be adapted for online or e-mailed questionnaires:

   a. Send a brief "prenotice" letter or e-mail saying that a questionnaire is coming. Prenotices are brief, personalized letters that inform a potential respondent that a questionnaire is coming and, when appropriate, what general issues are the focuses of the questionnaire.

b. Send the questionnaire with a clear cover letter. If you are conducting an online survey, you will need a brief cover letter that the respondent will read before filling out the questionnaire. The cover letter is a primary persuasive communication that should induce respondents to fill out your questionnaire. The cover letter should convey the following information:

- The date that the questionnaire was sent out and when the survey will close (so people who are away know whether they should even fill out the survey).
- What will happen (when the questionnaire will arrive and in what format).
- The general topic of the questionnaire.
- The rationale behind the questionnaire and, most importantly, how the respondent will benefit from the results of the survey. You are likely to get a higher response if you use user-focused phrasing in the invitation rather than organization-focused phrasing.
- A brief note about any incentives that will accompany the survey and how they will be delivered to the respondent (e.g., checks, PayPal, or online gift certificates).
- A thank you.
- A personal contact with e-mail and/or a phone number (and signature if mailed).

c. Send a thank you card or e-mail with a note stating, "There is still time to send the questionnaire back if you have not already sent it in." This is useful when you do not have a system that tracks who has and who has not responded to your survey invitation. More sophisticated systems can track who has not responded and target only those respondents.

d. Send a replacement questionnaire.

e. Make a final contact (preferably by another mode such as e-mail or phone).

3. **Personalize the survey.** The cover letter should include a specific person's name and title, not just a group name such as "Acme Corporation Satisfaction Committee." Here is an example:

Scott Smith
Senior Vice President, Product Engineering
ACME Software, Inc.
Wayland, MA

4. **Provide a way for respondents to contact you if they have questions.** Provide an e-mail, phone, or website with information about your group and a specific person who can answer questions about the survey. Many people worry about giving out a specific name and contact information, but this is a way to show trust and respect for your respondent, and if you have followed good principles of questionnaire design, very few people are likely to call. If you follow the advice in the previous step to have a high status person sign-off, you might want to have an e-mail alias (such as satisfaction.survey. feedback@acme.com) set up that will relay questions or comments to you, rather than the vice president (with his or her permission of course).

5. **If you will be putting your questionnaire online, a number of implementation details can improve your survey results** (Schonlau, Fricker, & Elliot, 2002):
   - Test your online survey with different operating systems, hardware (Mac, PC, tablet), browsers, resolutions, and connection speeds (especially slow speeds).
   - Be aware that mass e-mailings are sometimes being intercepted as spam by Internet service providers (ISPs). You might want to stagger your e-mailing somewhat. This author once sent out an e-mail survey request to 75 people through his ISP and unknowingly violated a spam/bulk e-mail policy, resulting in a loss of e-mail privileges and a serious fight to get those privileges back.

●●●

Legal Issues with Opt-in/Opt-out

If you are sending out large-scale surveys to your customers, check on your corporate policies regarding customer opt-in/opt-out requests. Some companies maintain a sales or marketing database that is tapped by different groups, including UX researchers and designers. Some databases may have a record of whether the customers want to receive different kinds of information, e.g., marketing literature, surveys, and product updates. If you send out a survey to customers who have opted out of receiving surveys, you may violate both company policy and state laws. For general information on laws related to opt-in/opt-out of e-mail material, see http://www.lsoft.com/resources/optinlaws.asp.

   - Provide a simple way for respondents to report problems with the survey. It is useful to include an e-mail address or phone number at the beginning and end of questionnaires.

* Consider whether respondents need a way to save partially completed surveys. Different online survey tools often have a setting that allows a person to save a partially completed survey and then return by clicking on the original link.
* Determine how much automatic validation you want to include in your survey. Do you want to force answers by having required questions or check for appropriate answers when you are using web or survey software?

●●●
―――

Required (Mandatory) Versus Optional Questions

Online survey tools provide a feature that allows you to set some questions as optional and some as required. Required questions stop the respondent from moving forward in a questionnaire and provide some cue that some choice or entry is needed. When you design survey questions, you must ask, "What is essential?" and make those essential questions required. Some categories of required questions include the following:

* Screening questions at the beginning of the survey that direct the respondent to a particular path in the questionnaire. Screening questions can include simple demographics such as job role or experience level.
* Conditional questions in a survey that direct the respondent to more detailed or specific questions (which may or may not be required).
* Essential questions that your team believes will provide the data needed to support hypotheses or make decisions. For example, in a customer satisfaction survey, you might have a set of questions relating to feature usability that will influence strategic or tactical planning.
* Critical open questions that asks respondents to enter text statements that provide details that are important for making decisions. For example, you may have a required open question as a follow-up to a satisfaction question.

Post-Survey Activities

After you send out your questionnaire, there are still a few things to do:

1. **Evaluate early returns to see if there are any problems that you did not notice in your questionnaire development.** Did any bugs crop up that you missed in your early reviews? Are you getting odd answers to a particular question? If your questionnaire is online, you might be able to fix the problem without losing too many respondents.

One thing you can do to check the entire system when you are doing online surveys is to choose a small sample of respondents, say 50–200, send the survey to that group, and examine the data that come back to see if there are any issues or any complaints by respondents. If there are no issues after 24 hours, then send the survey to your entire list of potential respondents.

2. **At planned times, send out reminders to people who have not yet filled out your questionnaire.** Some online systems track who has returned surveys (e.g., the Vovici online survey tool) which makes it easy to send reminders only to those who have not submitted their survey. If you cannot track who has submitted their survey, you can word your reminder message to indicate that because of privacy issues or limitations of the software everyone got a reminder, even if they have already submitted. If you have posted a survey on a wiki, website, social media site, or blog, then there will be no way to send reminders though you might post a note on the site before the end of the survey.

3. **Schedule adequate time for data analysis and interpretation.** Most online surveys have built-in tools that can support analysis, but interpreting the data and developing your conclusions can take time, especially with a large sample and a long questionnaire with many open-ended questions. One of the most common pitfalls of survey studies is to underestimate how long it takes to analyze and interpret the data.

4. **Note the limitations of the data or survey process in any reports or presentations.** Any report of the survey data should describe the sample and any limitations that might affect the validity of the results and interpretation. For example, if your sample is heavily biased toward only "good" customers or a particular industry out of several that use your product, then you should indicate those potential biases.

5. **Conduct a post-survey review with the product team.** Note how the survey design process worked and what you might do differently in terms of questionnaire and survey design.

VARYING AND EXTENDING QUESTIONNAIRES AND SURVEYS VIA MIXED-MODE SURVEYS

Mixed-mode surveys involve the use of different survey formats for asking questions on the same topic. For example, you might use a paper survey to gather data at a corporate conference and an online survey tool to get feedback from people who could not attend the conference. Possible formats include online surveys, mailed surveys, telephone surveys, face-to-face structured interviews, and interactive voice response (IVR) surveys (the kind that you often get at dinnertime from a phone polling group). The use of mixed modes is sometimes necessary in the following situations:

- You have different groups in your sample that may not have access to a particular survey mode (elderly users may not be comfortable with online or e-mail surveys and want a paper survey or a phone interview).
- You need to collect data during different situations where a mode may not be available (you do not have a computer, but you do have phone access to your respondents).
- Your respondents may not trust a particular mode.

Mixed-mode surveys can reduce costs and increase response rates (your beta users might be more willing to answer a set of questions on the phone than fill out a paper or online survey). The problem with using mixed-mode approaches is that different modes can yield different results. Dillman (2009) gives a number of examples where the same people answered questions in self-administered surveys differently from face-to-face interviews. If you plan mixed-mode surveys, then design the various questionnaires to be as similar as possible. Schonlau et al. (2002) describe case studies on mixed-mode surveys (e.g., online and e-mail) that might provide some useful tips for those contemplating the mixed approach. Dillman (2009) also provides some best practices for designing mixed-mode surveys, although he acknowledges that some of the principles are in need of additional research support.

MAJOR ISSUES IN THE USE OF QUESTIONNAIRES AND SURVEYS

There are some issues that often surface during the design and use of questionnaires and surveys. This section highlights some of these issues.

Using Questionnaires to Compare Products Against a Norm

Comparing products against a norm or benchmark requires considerable skill in psychometrics (the discipline of designing, administering, and interpreting quantitative tests dealing with attitudes and other psychological variables) because of the importance of establishing reliability and validity. Dumas (2003) notes that the development of a reliable and valid questionnaire for comparing products involves several steps:

1. **Conduct an item analysis to determine which questions are "good" and which are "bad."** An item analysis begins with the generation of a large number of questions that you believe relate to a concept, e.g., satisfaction with a product (Robson, 2002). After generating many items related to a concept, you create a pilot questionnaire with as many questions as possible and present it to a sample of the target respondents. Then you examine the results and look for questions where, for example, everyone agreed, disagreed, or gave the same answer. You eliminate these questions because they do not provide any discrimination. The next general step is to compare scores on each question against the overall score and eliminate questions that are not highly correlated with the overall score in order to increase the internal consistency of the questions and reduce random error. Finally, you revise your questionnaire with the remaining items, generate new items if necessary, and repeat the process of examining questions for discrimination and internal consistency. It may take several rounds of creating questions, pilot testing, analyzing, and revising a questionnaire before you have a good set of questions.

2. **Test the reliability of the questionnaire.** Several types of reliability tests can be used (Aiken, 2002; Bailey, 1994). One type, test-retest, involves giving the same set of respondents the same questions separated by enough time so that they would not remember their answers to the first questionnaire. One problem with test-retest reliability is determining the length of the interval between the two administrations of the questionnaire. If the interval is too short, the reliability (usually referred to as a reliability coefficient) may be inflated because of the effects of memory. On the other hand, if the interval is too long, then something may change that would lower the test-retest reliability coefficient. A second form of reliability is called "split-half" reliability where a single questionnaire contains two sets of questions designed to measure the same thing.
   The following practical factors can affect reliability:
   a. Ambiguous questions or response categories that lead respondents to interpret the questions differently.

b. Use of terms that are not understood by all respondents.

c. Double questions where it is not clear what part of the double question participants are responding to.

d. Differences in the administration of the questionnaire. (An assumption of psychometric questionnaires is that they will be administered under standard conditions, but this assumption may not hold in many circumstances.)

3. **Assess the validity of the questionnaire.** Reliability refers to consistency and stability; validity refers to the degree to which the questionnaire is measuring what it is supposed to measure—effectiveness, efficiency, satisfaction, or trustworthiness, for example. There are different types of validity, including the following (Campbell & Stanley, 1963; Cook & Campbell, 1979; Rosenthal & Rosnow, 2008):

a. *Content validity*: Does the questionnaire include content that is relevant to the purpose of the questionnaire? In general, content validity refers to the representativeness of the sample of questions relative to the entire domain of questions that could be chosen for the topic of interest (e.g., usability, satisfaction, quality).

b. *Criterion validity*: Do the results of the questionnaire correlate with subsequent outcomes such as sales figures or website hits?

c. *Convergent validity*: Do the results for one questionnaire correlate with the results of other questionnaires or methods that attempt to measure the same thing? For example, if you used the QUIS (Chin, Diehl, & Norman, 1988) and SUMI (Kirakowski & Corbett, 1993) questionnaires (both described later) to measure the subjective usability of a product, you might expect a fairly high correlation between the results because they both purport to measure the general usability of a product.

d. *Internal validity* (Campbell & Stanley, 1963): Internal validity deals with the confidence you place in the causal statements you make from a study. Internal validity can be influenced by a number of factors (Cook & Campbell, 1979), including mortality (people dropping out), history (a fire alarm goes off as you are administering a questionnaire), and instrumentation changes (a person conducting a structured interview based on a questionnaire becomes fatigued during the course of a long day and asks questions differently). At a practical level, internal validity focuses on factors that affect whether the results of an inquiry (a questionnaire study in this case) can be explained by other hypotheses. For example, imagine that you send out a customer satisfaction survey on the same day that the media announce that your product had a security loophole, and your customers' employee information might be in the hands of a spammer or worse. You get the surveys back, and it appears that people were less satisfied with the product than the previous year. The results might be due to real dissatisfaction or due to the announcement of the security hole and media attention.

  e. *External validity* (Campbell & Stanley, 1963): External validity refers to the generalizability of causal relationships. In a somewhat looser sense, external validity refers to the relevance of the findings in a wider context ("the real world"). External validity is compromised by poor or too highly focused samples of respondents, artificial settings (e.g., usability labs), and history.

4. **Develop standards and norms.** A final step in the development of psychometric questionnaires is to create norms regarding what is good and bad. For example, if you used a standardized tool to assess the subjective usability of your financial website, you might get a score of 78, but you would need to understand how your score compares to the scores of other similar financial websites.

Developing a standardized tool for assessing products on a particular psychological construct such as usability, pleasure, or satisfaction is a rigorous and time-consuming process requiring the assistance of a skilled psychometrician.

Wording of Questions

Dozens of common-sense guidelines are available on how to word survey questions (Dillman, 1978, 2000, 2007, 2009; Payne, 1951). The problem with these guidelines is that they can often be at odds with one another. For example, Dillman (2000, 2007) describes how the advice to "Use simple words" conflicts with the advice to "Keep questions short." The use of simple words or phrases (rather than a single complex word or short phrase) can increase the length of a question.

The application of common guidelines for questionnaire design must consider the background of respondents and context of the study. If you are designing questions for college professors who use web-based course software, you may not have to use simple, one or two syllable words. If you are sending out a web-based questionnaire to a general audience, then you might consider the use of simple words. Keep the context of your questionnaire study in mind when you are working on specific questions and applying these very general guidelines.

When you are crafting specific questions, you should consider the following wording guidelines. (Additional guidelines on the wording of questions can be found in Converse and Presser (1986), Salant and Dillman (1994), and the references by Dillman and his colleagues (2000, 2007, 2009).

1. **Choose words that will be understood by all your respondents.** A common mistake is to assume that everyone in your sample will understand technical terms, acronyms, and abbreviations. To be safe, avoid highly technical terms (usability, e.g., may not be understood by many people), acronyms, and abbreviations. For example, many of us may know what ISP, CMS, or ERP means, but our respondents may not, or worse still, pretend they do.

2. **Design questions so they address a single issue.** "Double questions"—two questions posing as a single question—are difficult to answer and should be split into two separate questions with the appropriate response alternatives. Double questions are a common mistake in the design of surveys and are often found even on surveys by market research firms. Here are examples of double questions that should be split into two questions.
   Example 1: "How usable and reliable is this system?"
   This first example is a double question because it asks one question about usability and a second question about reliability. Although there is often a connection between reliability and usability (if something crashes a lot, it might be viewed as unusable; on the other hand, it may be quite usable most of the time but crash once in a while), but this double question will produce muddled results. You would not know if you need to work on the UI, the underlying code, or both for improved reliability. Here is another example of a double question.
   Example 2: "How satisfied were you with the performance and usability of the BookBuyer.com website?"
   In this second example, the performance of the site might be great, but the usability is poor, or vice versa. This question can be split

into one question about performance and another question about usability. This type of mistake renders the data difficult to interpret because it is not clear which "question" (performance or usability) the participant is answering.

Fowler and Mangione (1990, p. 84) describe another category of double questions called "hidden questions" where an implied question is part of an explicit question. For example, the question "Who will you vote for in the next User Experience Professionals Association (UXPA) election?" has an implied question, "**Will you vote** in the next UXPA election?" and an explicit question, "**Who will you vote for** in the UXPA election?" The next time you fill out a questionnaire, keep a close eye out for double questions. They are far too common and lead to uninterpretable results.

3. **Avoid leading or biased questions.** Common types of leading questions begin with "Do you agree that....?" or "Rate how poor you found ...." The first example presumes that you agree with a statement, and the second one implies poor performance. Social desirability is another bias that can creep into questions. Social desirability is the tendency (conscious or unconscious) of people to give answers that they think will make them look good. Here is a simple example:

> **"Are you interested in obtaining another degree in the next 10 years?"**

Respondents might tend to check "Yes" because it is socially desirable to obtain an advanced degree and enhance your skill set. Moreover, the phrase "Are you interested" is a vague phrase—what does it mean "to be interested?" Perhaps "to be interested" means that you have another degree on your "bucket list" (the list of things that you want to do before you die) but is that a sufficient level of interest?

4. **Phrase questions positively.** Positive questions are generally easier to understand than negative questions (Akiyama, Brewer, & Shoben, 1979).

> **Poor:** Rate the degree to which the software you just used has no performance problem.

> **Better:** Rate the performance of the software you just used.

Converse and Presser (1986) warn that double negatives can sneak into questions with agree/disagree response categories when you ask respondents to state whether they agree or disagree with a negative statement, such as "Should paper documentation not be packaged with the software?" To say that documentation should be shipped with the software, you have to disagree which makes this a double negative. The use of negative questions can lead to response errors.

5. **Do not ask questions that are too specific or questions that exceed the cognitive capacities of most humans.** The "better" question in the following example reduces the interval in question from one year to one week—remembering how many times you did something over a year is asking too much. The responses here need to fit the particular time interval and can be based on pilot testing, interviews, or logging data of actual help usage from a sample of users.

Poor: About how many times in the last year did you use online Help? _____ Number of times

Better: About how many times in the last week did you use online Help? (Check one answer.)

☐ None
☐ 1–5
☐ 6–10
☐ 11 or more

Questionnaire and Question Length

An important part of the questionnaire design process is to determine how long it takes to fill out the questionnaire. This can be done during pilot testing. There are no strict guidelines for the length of a self-administered questionnaire (e.g., no more than two pages or ten questions in an online survey) because response rates will vary as a function of the relevance of the topic, the respondents' motivations, the quality of the survey, and the population that you are studying. Dillman (2000) reports on three experiments that looked at the length of mail questionnaires and found that greater length generally decreased response rates. He also found that a large postcard with two questions had virtually the same response rate as a legal size sheet with questions on both sides. Dillman (2000) suggests that very short questionnaires might be viewed as not very meaningful by respondents. Bailey (1994) reported on a study by Scott that compared one and two page versions of the same paper questionnaire to explore the impact of "question density" and found no statistical difference in response rates (the two-page questionnaire had a response rate of 94.8% while the one-page version had a response rate of 93.6%). Yammarino et al. (1991) conducted a meta-analysis of mail response behavior and concluded that mail survey responses could be raised by using questionnaires that were less than four pages; surveys longer than four pages yielded lower response rates.

Here are several general guidelines that you might consider when discussing the length of your questionnaire as it relates to response rates:

- If you provide a statement about how long it will take to complete the survey ("This survey will take less than 5 minutes to complete"), make sure that your statement is reasonable.
- Keep in mind that the more questions you have, the less time your respondents might spend on each item.
- Make sure that every item relates to a research and business goal.
- If you do not have a plan on how to analyze a question, leave it out. Do not be tempted to piggyback questions without a clear purpose.
- Do not make your questionnaire so brief (e.g., postcards with two to three questions) that your respondents view it as meaningless.
- Keep questions short, but keep in mind the trade-off of question length versus the use of simple words (more simple words may improve comprehension but add to length).
- Break a long list of questions into subgroups.
- Avoid the tendency to squeeze questions together so tightly that the question density is analogous to the density of a neutron star. Cramming questions together to cut down the number of pages can result in a cluttered, complex appearance.
- Consider the motivation of your respondents. If your respondents are highly motivated, for example, they are part of a dedicated customer council for your product, then you can consider longer questionnaires.
- Consider some incentive for completing the survey.

Recall and Memory

Questionnaire respondents are often asked to recall events that occurred days, weeks, or months in the past. The main factors affecting recall questions are elapsed time, the vividness of events, and the frequency of events that compete with the specific events that the respondent is asked to recall (Foddy, 1993). General guidelines for minimizing recall problems and other memory biases include the following (Dillman, 2000, 2007; Sudman, Bradburn, & Schwarz, 1996):

- Provide memory cues to aid recall. Rather than asking respondents to list what they do during a day in an open question, you can list primary activities as well as allow the respondent to add ones missing from the list of answers.
- Provide a reasonable time period for recall questions. This requires some knowledge of the relative frequency of the activity of interest. If you are asking about training, you might ask how much training the respondent had in the past six months rather than in the past month because training is a relatively rare event in some organizations.
- Ask the respondent to refer to personal calendars, diaries, or other memory aids that could improve the completeness and accuracy of recall questions.
- Ask respondents to work in chronological order backward.

Ordering of Questions

Most questionnaires ask respondents to answer more than a single question, which means that designers must consider how to order the questions. Determining the "best" order of questions is complex because earlier questions are likely to influence later questions in ways that are hard to predict (Dillman, 2000; Foddy, 1993; Sudman, Bradburn, & Schwarz, 1996). For example, asking specific questions about the usability of a product at the beginning of a survey could "prime" a person to answer general questions that follow in a particular way. For a good summary of potential order effects in questionnaire design, see Dillman (2000, pp. 86–94).

A number of ordering schemes have been formulated for questionnaires. In most cases, questionnaires use a mix of these ordering schemes. Here are three general approaches for ordering questions:

1. **Funnel approach.** The first approach for ordering questions is often called the "funnel" or "general-to-specific" approach. In the funnel approach, the questionnaire designer begins with general, but relatively simple and nonthreatening open-ended and closed questions first. Then the questions become more and more specific. The funnel approach is reasonable if the early general questions are easy to

answer and relevant. This approach can fail if you ask open questions early in the questionnaire that require substantial effort, such as "Describe, in as much detail as possible, your use of [Product X]." This is not a good opening question!

2. **Inverted funnel approach.** The second approach is to go from specific to general questions (the "inverted funnel"). One rationale for this approach is that the specific questions in the beginning will get the respondent to think about the topic and be more primed to answer subsequent general questions.

3. **Logical order.** The last general approach is to present items in some logical order. A logical order may be a time sequence (if you want to get information on tasks and activities in a typical day), a functional sequence, or some other logical order.

Most questionnaires incorporate several of the general ordering approaches. You might use a logical order by topic, but within a particular subset of questions, go from general to specific or follow a timeline. Table 2.7 presents more specific guidelines for question ordering.

Table 2.7 Guidelines for Ordering Questions	
Guideline	**Discussion**
Choose the first question wisely.	Dillman (2000) and Bailey (1994) stress that the first question is the most crucial one in a questionnaire and is likely to determine whether a person responds to additional questions. Consider designing the first question so that it has the following traits: • **Easy to understand.** • **Easy to answer.** Consider a factual question with limited response categories that *everyone* can answer. • **Interesting and relevant.** The respondent should feel that the first question is worth answering. • **Clearly connected to the purpose of the questionnaire.** • **Nonthreatening.** Do not start out by asking a question that would threaten the respondent. Even a question as simple as "How often do you use [Product X]?" could be threatening if it is a product they are supposed to use every day but do not.
Put demographic questions at the end of the survey.	While demographic questions may be quite relevant to the survey team, they are not very relevant to the respondent. Dillman (2000) notes that many questionnaire designers want to start out with a question about education or age or job title, but these may not be connected to the purpose of the survey. Demographic questions (other than screening questions) should go at the end of most questionnaires. The exception here is if you need to ask some demographics (e.g., role or age) to screen participants or to have them take a different path through the survey.
Group related questions and identify the grouping with a header.	This sounds obvious but is often forgotten during design. In addition to the physical grouping of related questions, consider a heading that explicitly identifies logical groups.

(Continued)

Table 2.7 (Continued)	
Guideline	**Discussion**
Group questions that have similar response formats.	If you have questions that have similar formats (yes/no; rating scales, agree/disagree statements) within a particular logical group, consider placing them together to ease the cognitive burden on the respondent who would not have to think about how to answer different response formats.
Put any threatening questions at the end (or mix them in with less threatening questions).	This is common advice in questionnaire manuals, and if you are doing research into drugs, crime, sex, or related activities, it might be obvious what constitutes a threatening question. The concept of "threatening" can be somewhat more subtle in UCD questionnaires. The following are some less obvious items that can threaten respondents: • Questions that get into how people "really" do things as opposed to how they are supposed to do them. Admitting shortcuts at work could get the respondents in trouble with managers who eschew shortcuts or corporate policies that require a different approach. • Questions that ask about training and experience. • Questions that reflect security or privacy concerns. Asking questions about how people remember passwords can be extremely threatening. • Questions about income and age. • Questions about problems at work that are directed at international respondents who might consider it improper to talk about work problems with strangers. It may not be possible to put all threatening questions at the end of a survey, so you should consider ways to get the information you need by reducing the threat. For example, questions about income can include broad response categories (0−20,000, 20,001−50,000, ...) rather than asking: "What is your income? _____ Dollars"

GUIDELINES FOR DESIGNING RESPONSE CATEGORIES

Response categories are the answer choices that you provide to respondents. Many guidelines are available about how to design response categories. Some of the important guidelines are listed here. Additional guidelines can be found in Dillman (2000), Robson (2002), and other books on survey and questionnaire design.

1. **Response categories should be mutually exclusive (and exhaustive).** If your categories overlap, it will be hard to interpret the data. The obvious example of overlapping categories can often be seen in age questions where you have response categories such as 20−30, 30−40, 40−50, 50−60, 60−70, and 70 and over. Dillman notes that this seemingly minor overlap at the boundaries is bothersome to those whose age falls at the boundary for a paper or online survey. A more subtle form of categories that are not mutually exclusive occurs when you mix textual responses with two or more dimensions. Here is an example where general sources (magazines and newspapers) are mixed with specific delivery techniques (online, friend or colleague, e-mail alerts).

Poor: Where do you get information about new computer products?

___ Magazines
___ Newspapers
___ Online
___ Friend or colleague
___ E-mail alerts
___ *PC Magazine*

It is possible that the magazines and newspapers are online versions rather than paper versions so those two response categories could overlap with the "Online" response. You can make the responses more specific to reduce the overlap:

Better: Where do you get information about new computer products?

___ Online magazines
___ *PC Magazine* (hardcopy)
___ Online newspapers
___ Paper newspaper
___ Blogs or wikis
___ Friend or colleague
___ E-mail alerts
___ Other: _____

2. **Avoid vague response quantifiers when more precise quantifiers can be used.** In Example 1a, the response categories are vague and can be interpreted differently by respondents. The data from this question would be nearly impossible to interpret (what does "occasionally" mean?). Example 1b eliminates the vague quantifiers with more specific answers.

Poor: 1a. How often did you use Product X during the past month? (Check one answer.)

___ Never
___ Rarely
___ Occasionally
___ Regularly

Better: 1b. How often did you use Product X during the past month? (Check one answer.)

___ Not at all
___ 1−3 times a month
___ Once a week
___ 2−4 times a week

___ Once a day

___ More than once a day

3. **Keep the space constant for response categories.** Making some categories larger than others might lead to the impression that one category is more important than another (see examples in Table 2.8 and Table 2.9). This can be somewhat difficult for web questionnaires that are on pages that can be resized. Developers need to design response categories so the size of each category is fixed or the categories expand evenly when the page size is changed.

Table 2.8 Poor—the Disagree and Strongly Disagree Response Cells Are Larger Than the Others				
Strongly Agree	Agree	Undecided	Disagree	Strongly Disagree
		X		

Table 2.9 Better—All the Response Cells Have the Same Spacing				
Strongly Agree	Agree	Undecided	Disagree	Strongly Disagree
	X			

●●●

Reducing the Number of Response Categories to Accommodate Multiple Screen Sizes

If you will be presenting questions on small mobile devices, you might consider using three- point or five-point scales rather than seven- or nine-point scales.

4. **Whenever possible, avoid multiple columns of responses.** Use a vertical list rather than a horizontal list. Some respondents might miss the last column or assume that you need to choose one item in each column.

Poor: Triple-column approach:

☐ Item 1	☐ Item 4	☐ Item 7
☐ Item 2	☐ Item 5	☐ Item 8
☐ Item 3	☐ Item 6	☐ Item 9

Better: Single-column approach:

☐ Item 1
☐ Item 2
☐ Item 3
☐ Item 4
☐ Item 5
☐ Item 6
☐ Item 7
☐ Item 8
☐ Item 9

Rating Scales

Several major types of rating scales are used in survey questions. This section highlights major types of rating scales and some of the issues that you need to consider when choosing these scales. For more details on how to choose and design rating scales see Rosnow and Rosenthal (2013), Aiken (2002), and Robson (2002). William W. K. Trochim, a professor at Cornell, has a good summary of scaling methods at http://www.socialresearchmethods.net/kb/scaling.php.

Arbitrary Scaling

Some of the ratings scales might be "arbitrary" because they are based on a researcher's assumptions about what items will measure a particular concept like satisfaction or usability. Arbitrary ratings scales are often developed when a usability practitioner gets a call to create a quick and dirty survey to find out why people seem to be complaining about a product. This harried practitioner will pull together a set of questions with rating scales that have some face validity—they seem like they should measure the concept—but in reality have not been objectively validated in any way.

Likert Scaling

Likert scales, also called summated ratings, most commonly ask users to rate their agreement or disagreement with a set of 20–30 statements that have been derived from pretesting and item analysis (Robson, 2002). Here is an example of a Likert item:

Working with this website is satisfying. (Choose one answer).

___ *Strongly Agree*

___ *Agree*

___ *Neutral*

___ *Disagree*

___*Strongly Disagree*

The scales in the SUMI questionnaires (Kirakowski, 2000) use three response categories (different numbers of alternatives are allowed for Likert scales, and alternative labels are also permitted). Kirakowski has documented the process for developing the SUMI Likert scale in detail at http://www.ucc.ie/hfrg/questionnaires/sumi/sumipapp.html# sumidev.

	Agree	Undecided	Disagree
The instructions and prompts are helpful.	☐	☐	☐

One of the problems with many surveys that appear to use Likert scaling is that there is no systematic process for generating and analyzing the statements that are included in the questionnaire. Robson (2002) describes Likert-looking scales that did not go through the Likert development process as arbitrary scales and proclaims:

It is still distressingly common to see scales cobbled together by assembling an arbitrary group of statements which sound as if they would be relevant, with similarly 'off the top of the head' ratings assigned to different answers, and a simple addition of these ratings to obtain some mystical 'attitude score'.

If you want to develop your own Likert scale, consider collaborating with a statistician or psychometrician because there are important considerations in this analysis, including the distributional properties of each item (skewness, kurtosis). The shape of the curves for each item will influence whether parametric or nonparametric methods should be used. The general process for developing a Likert scale involves the following general steps (Robson, 2002).

1. Gather a large number of items that appear to be related to an issue. These statements might come from other surveys, brainstorming, articles about the product, usability reviews, and other sources.

You should collect positive and negative items and avoid extreme statements because they will not discriminate among respondents. You should have about equal numbers of positive and negative statements.

2. Decide how you will categorize the responses. The most common approach is to use five categories: strongly disagree, disagree, undecided, agree, and strongly agree. Values of 1 through 5 are assigned to these items. When you are analyzing data, the most positive value is assigned a "5." If your item is phrased negatively ("This product is hard to use"), strong disagreement would be a good thing, so here you would assign a "5" to the strongly disagree answer.

3. Administer a trial questionnaire with Likert items. Ask a large number of respondents who are similar to your target population to rate their agreement/disagreement with the collection of positive and negative statements about a particular attitude object.

4. Calculate a total score for each respondent by adding the values of all the responses. Rank the participants based on their total score on all the items. This would give you an ordered list from most to least favorable. This ranking will be used in selecting which items will be used in the final questionnaire

5. Use an item analysis to choose the most discriminating items for the final set of items. There are different approaches to choosing items. You can calculate how well the items discriminate between the upper and the lower quartiles (Robson, 2002, pp. 294−295) or choose the items that correlate most highly with the overall scores. The least discriminating items are removed from the questionnaire.

●●●
_____

You Pronounce Likert as "LICK-ert," not "LIKE-ert"

Nearly everyone pronounces Likert as "Like-ert," but Tullis and Albert (2008) and Babbie (2005, p. 174) note that Dr. Rensis Likert, the developer of Likert scales, pronounced his name as "Lick-ert."
_____

Semantic Differential Scales

The widely used semantic differential scale (Osgood, Suci, & Tannenbaum, 1957) is used to assess subjective meaning of a concept to respondents (see an example in Table 2.10). The semantic differential scale presents respondents with a set of bipolar scales (good/bad, helpful/ unhelpful, useless/valuable). Respondents are asked to choose a number

Table 2.10 Sample Semantic Differential Scales								
Attractive	1	2	3	4	5	6	7	Unattractive
Unhelpful	1	2	3	4	5	6	7	Helpful
Friendly	1	2	3	4	5	6	7	Unfriendly
Simple	1	2	3	4	5	6	7	Complex

(generally 1−7) or check the position on an unnumbered scale that indicates the extent to which the adjectives relate to a word or phrase. For example, you might be asked to rate a software product on the following bipolar dimensions by circling the number that represents your subjective judgment of that product on each bipolar dimension.

Thurstone Scaling (Equal-Appearing Intervals)

Thurstone scaling uses statements themselves to represent scale values that range from highly favorable to neutral to highly unfavorable. The creation of a Thurstone scale is laborious in that you have to create 50−100 statements that are worded similarly and then have those statements sorted by a large number of "judges" on an 11-point scale from 1 (least favorable to the concept) to 11 (most favorable to the concept). The judges must rate the favorableness of each statement in terms of an attitude toward that concept; judges are not to rate the statements based on their own opinions. After the judges do their ratings, the medians and inter-quartile ranges of each statement are calculated, and then the items are sorted on their median values. From this sorted list, statements are chosen that have equal intervals across the range of medians. These statements are then put into a format where respondents can agree or disagree with them. The actual measure of attitudes toward the target concept is determined by adding the scale values of all the items marked "agree."

Hundreds of studies have been conducted on ratings scales, many of them producing conflicting results. More details about the types of scales, validation issues, biases, and problems can be found in Trochim (2006), Robson (2002), and other websites, books, and articles dealing with attitude measurement.

Questionnaire Layout

The design of self-administered paper or online questionnaires can affect response rates (Dillman, Sinclair, & Clark, 1993) and measurement errors (missing questions, improperly answered questions). Dillman (2000) notes that good design makes surveys more interesting, credible, and easy to fill out. Here is a summary of questionnaire layout guidelines:

- Build a good information organization into the questionnaire.
- Put instructions right where they are needed. The often used set of general instructions at the beginning of a questionnaire those should never substitute for clear instructions with each question.
- Use visual cues to differentiate instructions, questions, and response categories. For example, you could put instructions in parentheses, bold the questions, and use normal text (unbolded) for the response categories. Whatever style you choose should be used consistently throughout. Following is an example using bold for the question, parentheses for the instruction, and normal text plus indenting for the response categories. Other approaches would work just as well, but the point is that when a person looks at a page or screen, the different types of information stand out clearly.

  1. **How often did you use Product X during the past month?** (Check one answer.)
     __ Not at all
     __ 1–3 times a month
     __ Once a week
     __ 2–4 times a week
     __ Once a day
     __ More than once a day

- List response categories vertically instead of horizontally. Vertical response categories are easier to scan.
- Avoid double banking of response options, especially if they are of the "Check all that apply" type. Some respondents may think that they need to check something in each column.
- Consider where you place the selection box for responses. If you are doing an online survey, it may be easier to put the selection box on the left of the item. If you are doing a paper survey, you might put the box to the right of the item.

See Dillman (2000, 2007) for a detailed summary of questionnaire layout principles and research.

Rewards and Incentives

You can use a variety of incentives to increase response rates. Possible incentives include the following:

- Token financial incentives (cash or check) that are part of a package or are given when the questionnaire is returned.
- Material incentives such as pens, small pads, or other small gifts.
- Information incentives such as summary reports or the location of a website where the results will be posted.

Kuniavsky (2003, p. 328) notes that the choice of incentive will depend on knowing your audience. If you are looking for input from teenagers or geeky 54-year-old physics majors, the chance of winning a Sony PlayStation or Nikon digital camera, respectively, might boost response rates for online surveys. A common incentive is to run a lottery where a respondent has one chance to win a financial or material incentive such as a PDA or savings bond, but survey designers need to be cautious because there are often detailed legal requirements in different states and countries about sweepstake or lottery offers (Kuniavsky, 2003). Consult a lawyer if you plan a lottery as part of your incentive plan.

Weblink

For some additional information on using incentives for surveys, see http://www.polarismr.com/Portals/58820/newsletters/survey_sampling/ MRP_0105_Survey_Sweepstakes.htm and http://apps.americanbar.org/ buslaw/blt/2006-07-08/abrahamson.shtml.

Dillman (2000) summarizes research on incentives and concludes that it is generally worthwhile (it will increase response rates) to use a modest cash incentive ($1−5). The research indicates that small material gifts have less impact than cash. Dillman cites research showing that lotteries may not be very effective at invoking the norm of reciprocity (Gouldner, 1960), although this might vary with the specific type of lottery award. Promising people that they will receive cash or a gift when they return surveys does not seem to be very effective.

DATA ANALYSIS

Now that you understand the major issues involved in using questionnaires and surveys, it is time to consider how to analyze the data you will acquire. The range of analysis techniques for questionnaires is immense and a detailed discussion is beyond the scope of this chapter, but this author will briefly describe some of the basic types.

Following is a brief description of some of the basic types of data and analysis.

Types of Data

These are the basic data types from questionnaires:

- Response rates
- Subjective ratings and rankings
- Frequency data from unordered choice questions
- Textual data from open-ended questions
- Feedback about the questionnaire itself

Analysis Techniques

The questionnaire data just listed can be analyzed in many ways. Here are some of the more common techniques.

Qualitative Analysis of Open-Ended Data

Open-ended data can be broken down into text units and then sorted into themes or categories using affinity diagramming or qualitative analysis tools such as HyperRESEARCH or NVivo. These tools allow you to create a coding scheme that you can apply to qualitative data. Some tools can code text automatically by scanning for particular words or phrases. Suppose you had collected open-ended data in a customer satisfaction survey and had 500 responses to a question such as "What aspects of the product were most troublesome?" You could then code those responses by hand or automatically into categories such as "performance," "lack of tools," "compatibility," and "errors." After you have put the text into categories, you can extract frequencies from the text data and plot the frequencies of each category.

Exploratory Data Analysis

The branch of statistics called exploratory data analysis (EDA), which emerged in the 1970s, uses simple visual summaries of data and quantitative techniques to suggest hypotheses that can be tested. Tukey (1977) considered EDA exploratory rather than confirmatory. Tools of EDA include the following:

- Box plots
- Histograms
- Pareto diagrams
- Scatterplots

- Stem-and-leaf plots
- Median polish
- Multidimensional scaling

Some of the EDA tools, such as scatterplots and histograms, are fairly common in UCD research; however, other tools that are simple and powerful, such as box plots and stem-and-leaf plots, have not yet become mainstream tools for those working in UCD.

Frequency Counts
This is perhaps the simplest form of data analysis. For questions based on frequencies, you can create frequency tables or histograms to show the frequency of responses. These counts can reveal some general trends and are often the first thing that an investigator does with categorical data. Some survey software will tabulate frequency data as your surveys roll in. A histogram on frequency data can reveal how your data are distributed: normal, bi-modal, skewed, or oddly shaped.

Measures of Central Tendency, Variability, and Shape
Most reports of survey data contain measures of central tendency—most often the mean and standard deviation. Depending on the size of the data, it is sometimes useful to see values for both the mean and the median because differences between the mean and the median will indicate that the data are skewed negatively or positively. Skewness is an indicator of the asymmetry of a data set. If the data are positively skewed, then there is an elongated tail on the right side of a distribution; negatively skewed data yield an elongated tail on the left side of a distribution. The more skewed a distribution, the more the data depart from a normal distribution. If data are heavily skewed, the median might be a more appropriate measure of central tendency because the median is not affected as much by extreme data values as the mean.

Cross Tabulations
Cross tabulations (also called cross tabs or PivotTables in Excel) involve comparisons between two different sets of frequency data. Cross tabulations are most effective when the comparison does not involve too many categories. The simplest form of a cross tab is a 2×2 table like Table 2.11 based on the accompanying frequency table. As part of your planning you might have research issues that involve comparisons between questions. For example, you might want to

compare how often a person uses a website with what his or her goals are when using the site. So you would have a table comparing frequency of visits to a website with personal goals (look for information, create questionnaires, purchase household items, get DVDs).

●●●──

Detailed Guidance on Analysis Techniques

For more detailed guidance on analysis techniques consult the following books:

- Tullis, T., & Albert, B. (2008). *Measuring the user experience: Collecting, analyzing, and presenting usability metrics.* Morgan Kaufmann.
- Sauro, J. (2010). *A practical guide to measuring usability: 72 answers to the most common questions about quantifying the usability of websites and software.* Denver, CO: Measuring Usability.
- Sauro, J., & Lewis, J. R. (2012). *Quantifying the user experience: Practical statistics for user research.* Morgan Kaufmann.

Table 2.11 Frequency Table and Cross Tabulation of Gender by Age Category		
Participant	**Age Category**	**Gender**
1	<21	F
2	21–65	F
3	Over 65	M
4	21–65	M
5	21–65	F
6	21–65	M
7	<21	M
8	<21	M
9	21–65	M
10	Over 65	M

Age Category	Male	Female	
<21	2	1	3
	(20%)	(10%)	(30%)
21–65	3	2	5
	(30%)	(20%)	(50%)
Over 65	2	0	2
	(20%)	(0%)	(20%)
	7	3	10
	(70%)	(30%)	(100%)

RECOMMENDED READINGS

Dillman, D. A., Smyth, J. D., & Christian, L. M. (2009). *Internet, mail, and mixed-mode surveys: The tailored design method* (3rd ed.). Hoboken, NJ: Wiley. This is perhaps the best and most comprehensive book on survey design. This is the latest book from Don Dillman, a guru of questionnaire and survey design. Dillman's book is full of practical advice backed up by decades of research.

Sauro, J. (2010). *A practical guide to measuring usability: 72 answers to the most common questions about quantifying the usability of websites and software.* Denver, CO: Measuring Usability.

Sauro, J., & Lewis, J. R. (2012). *Quantifying the user experience: Practical statistics for user research.* Waltham, MA: Morgan Kaufmann.

Sudman, S., Bradburn, N. M., & Schwarz, N. (1996). *Thinking about answers: The application of cognitive processes to survey methodology.* San Francisco, CA: Jossey-Bass.

REFERENCES

Aiken, L. R. (2002). *Attitudes and related psychosocial constructs: Theories, assessment, and research.* Thousand Oaks, CA: Sage Publications.

Akiyama, M. M., Brewer, W. f., & Shoben, E. J. (1979). The yes/no question answering system and statement verification. *Journal of Verbal Learning and Verbal Behavior, 18*, 365–380.

Allison, P. D. (2001). *Missing data. Sage University paper series on quantitative applications in the social sciences, 07-136.* Thousand Oaks, CA: Sage Publications.

Atlas, M. (1981). The user edit: Making manuals easier to use. *IEEE Transactions on Professional Communication, 24*(1), 28–29.

Atlas, M. (1998). The user edit revisited, or "if we're so smart, why ain't we rich?". *Journal of Computer Documentation, 22*(3), 21–24.

Babbie, E. R. (2005). *The basics of social research.* Belmont, CA: Thomson Wadsworth.

Bailey, K. D. (1994). *Methods of social research* (4th ed.). New York, NY: The Free Press.

Blau, P. M. (1964). *Exchange and power in social life.* New York, NY: Wiley.

Bradburn, N. M., Sudman, S., & Wansink, B. (2004). *Asking questions: The definitive guide to questionnaire design—for market research, political polls, and social and health questionnaires (rev. ed.).* San Francisco, CA: Jossey-Bass.

Campbell, D., & Stanley, J. (1963). *Experimental and quasi-experimental designs for research.* Chicago, IL: Rand-McNally.

Charlton, S. G. (2002). Questionnaire techniques for test and evaluation in charlton. In G. Samuel, & T. G. O'Brien (Eds.), *Handbook of human factors testing and evaluation* (2nd ed., pp. 225–246). Mahwah, NJ: Lawrence Erlbaum Associates, Publishers.

Chin, J. P., Diehl, V. A., & Norman, K. L. (1988). *Development of an instrument measuring user satisfaction of the human–computer interface* (213–218). *Proceedings of CHI'88: Human factors in computing systems.* New York, NY: ACM.

Cialdini, R. B. (2001). *Influence: Science and practice* (4th ed.). Boston, MA: Allyn & Bacon.

Converse, J. M., & Presser, S. (Eds.), (1986). *Sage university paper series on quantitative applications in the social sciences, 07-063* Thousand Oaks, CA: Sage Publications.

Cook, T. D., & Campbell, D. T. (1979). *Quasi-experimentation: Design and analysis issues for field settings.* Boston, MA: Houghton Mifflin Company.

Dillman, D. A. (1978). *Mail and telephone surveys: The total design method.* New York, NY: Wiley.

Dillman, D. A. (2000). *Mail and internet surveys: The tailored design method* (2nd ed.). New York, NY: Wiley.

Dillman, D. A. (2007). *Mail and internet surveys: The tailored design* (2nd ed.). New York, NY: Wiley.

Dillman, D. A., Sinclair, M. D., & Clark, J. R. (1993). Effects of questionnaire length, respondent-friendly design, and a difficult question on response rates for occupant-addressed census mail surveys. *Public Opinion Quarterly, 57,* 289–304.

Dillman, D. A., Smyth, J. D., & Christian, L. M. (2009). *Internet, mail, and mixed-mode surveys: The tailored design method* (3rd ed.). Hoboken, NJ: Wiley.

Dumas, J. S. (2003). User-based evaluations. In J. K. Jacko, & A. Sears (Eds.), The human–computer interaction handbook. Manhwah, NJ: Lawrence Erlbaum Associates, Inc.

Foddy, W. (1993). *Constructing questions for interviews and questionnaires: Theory and practice in social research.* Cambridge, UK: Cambridge University Press.

Fowler, F. J., Jr., & Mangione, T. W. (1990). *Standardized survey interviewing: Minimizing interviewer-related error.* Newbury Park, CA: Sage Publications.

Galton, F. (1874). *English men of science: Their nature and nurture.* London: Macmillan.

Gouldner, A. W. (1960). The norm of reciprocity: A preliminary statement. *American Sociological Review, 25,* 161–178.

Groves, R. M., Fowler, F. J., Jr., Coupter, M. P., Lepkowski, J. M., Singer, E., & Tourangeau, R. (2009). *Survey methodology* (2nd ed.). New York, NY: Wiley.

Homans, G. C. (1958). Social behavior as exchange. *American Journal of Sociology, 63,* 597–606.

Kirakowski, J. (2000). Questionnaires in usability engineering: A list of frequently asked questions. In R. A. Krueger, & M. A. Casey (Eds.), *Focus groups: A practical guide for applied research* (3rd ed.). Thousand Oaks, CA: Sage Publications.

Kirakowski, J., & Corbett, M. (1993). SUMI: The software usability measurement inventory. *British Journal of Educational Technology, 24,* 210–212.

Krueger, R. A., & Casey, M. A. (2000). *Focus groups: A practical guide for applied research* (3rd ed.). Thousand Oaks, CA: Sage Publications.

Kuniavsky, M. (2003). *Observing the user experience: A practitioner's guide to user research.* San Francisco, CA: Morgan Kaufmann.

Langford, J., & McDonagh, D. (Eds.), (2003). *Focus groups: Supporting effective product development* Boca Raton, FL: CRC Press.

Levy, P. S., & Lemeshow, S. (1999). *Sampling of populations: Methods and applications* (3rd ed.). New York, NY: Wiley.

Lohr, S. L. (1999). *Sampling: Design and analysis.* Pacific Grove, CA: Duxbury Press.

McBurney, D. H. (1998). *Research methods* (4th ed.). Pacific Grove, CA: Brooks/Cole Publishing.

Meister, D. (1985). *Behavioral analysis and measurement methods.* New York, NY: Wiley.

Nemeth, C. O. (2004). *Human factors methods for design: Making systems human-centered.* Boca Raton, FL: CRC Press.

Osgood, C. E., Suci, G. J., & Tannenbaum, P. H. (1957). *The measurement of meaning.* Chicago, IL: University of Illinois Press.

Payne, S. L. (1951). *The art of asking questions.* Princeton, NJ: Princeton University Press.

Robson, C. (2002). *Real-world research* (2nd ed.). Malden, MA: Blackwell Publishing.

Rosenthal, R., & Rosnow, R. L. (2008). Essentials of behavioral research: Methods and data analysis (*3rd ed.*). New York, NY: McGraw-Hill.

Rosnow, R. L., & Rosenthal, R. (2013). *Beginning behavioral research: A conceptual primer* (7th ed.). Boston, MA: Pearson.

Salant, P., & Dillman, D. A. (1994). *How to conduct your own survey*. New York, NY: Wiley.

Sauro, J. (2010). *A practical guide to measuring usability: 72 answers to the most common questions about quantifying the usability of websites and software*. Denver, CO: Measuring Usability.

Sauro, J., & Lewis, J. R. (2012). *Quantifying the user experience: Practical statistics for user research*. Waltham, MA: Morgan Kaufmann.

Schonlau, M., Fricker, R., & Elliott, M. (2002). *Conducting research surveys via E-Mail and the web*. Santa Monica, CA: RAND.

Soderston, C. (1985). The user edit: A new level. *Technical Communication* 16—18 1st Quarter.

Sudman, S., Bradburn, N. M., & Schwarz, N. (1996). *Thinking about answers: The application of cognitive processes to survey methodology*. San Francisco, CA: Jossey-Bass.

Thibaut, J. W., & Kelley, H. H. (1959). *The social psychology of groups*. New York, NY: Wiley.

Trochim, W.M.K. (2006). *Scaling*. Retrieved from http://www.socialresearchmethods.net/kb/scaling.php June 26, 2013.

Tukey, J. W. (1977). *Exploratory data analysis*. Reading, MA: Addison-Wesley.

Tullis, T., & Albert, B. (2008). *Measuring the user experience: Collecting, analyzing, and presenting usability metrics*. Burlington, MA: Morgan Kaufmann.

Wilson, C. (2013). *Brainstorming and beyond: A user-centered design method*. Waltham, MA: Morgan Kaufmann.

Yammarino, F. J., Skinner, S. J., & Childers, T. L. (1991). Understanding mail survey response behavior: A meta-analysis. *Public Opinion Quarterly*, *55*, 613—639.

Standard Usability Questionnaires

Questionnaire Names: SUS, QUIS™, ASQ, PSSUQ, SUMI, WAMMI

Related Methods: Critical incident technique, questionnaires and surveys, structured interviews

OVERVIEW OF STANDARD USABILITY QUESTIONNAIRES

Standard usability questionnaires are data-collection tools that research groups have created and made available to the public either free (e.g., the System Usability Scale (SUS)) or at a reasonable licensing fee.

This appendix describes seven usability questionnaires that various groups or individuals with backgrounds in usability or human factors have developed to assess user reactions of the usability of a product. The descriptions of the commercial products may be brief because of proprietary information, but sources are provided for you to find additional information. The questionnaires covered in this appendix are given in Table A.1.

In the first part of this appendix, the focus is on free public domain questionnaires; in the second part, the focus is on commonly cited commercial or restricted questionnaires.

FREE SURVEYS

System Usability Scale
The SUS is a simple, 10-item questionnaire (Table A.2) that was designed at Digital Equipment Corporation by John Brooke in the mid-1980s to assess a user's overall satisfaction with a product (Brook, n.d.; Brooke, 1996; Sauro, 2011). The SUS questionnaire can be used without cost as long as the source of the questionnaire is acknowledged by the investigator (Brooke, 1996).

Table A.1 Standard Usability Questionnaires

SUS	System Usability Scale
ASQ	After Scenario Questionnaire
PSSUQ	Post Study System Usability Questionnaire
CSUQ	Computer System Usability Questionnaire
QUIS™	Questionnaire for User Satisfaction
SUMI	Software Usability Measurement Inventory
WAMMI	Website Analysis and Measurement Inventory

Table A.2 The 10-Item SUS Questionnaire

	Strongly Disagree				Strongly Agree
1. I think that I would like to use this system frequently.	1	2	3	4	5
2. I found the system unnecessarily complex.	1	2	3	4	5
3. I thought the system was easy to use.	1	2	3	4	5
4. I think that I would need the support of a technical person to be able to use this system.	1	2	3	4	5
5. I found the various functions in this system were well integrated.	1	2	3	4	5
6. I thought there was too much inconsistency in this system.	1	2	3	4	5
7. I would imagine that most people would learn to use this system very quickly.	1	2	3	4	5
8. I found the system very cumbersome to use.	1	2	3	4	5
9. I felt very confident using the system.	1	2	3	4	5
10. I needed to learn a lot of things before I could get going with this system.	1	2	3	4	5

The SUS covers a number of aspects of usability, including learning, consistency, training, integration, and complexity. The individual statements used in the SUS are based on a Likert scale obtained by conducting an item analysis of more than 50 items (Brooke, 1996) and examining which items discriminated a usable system from an unusable system.

Strengths of the SUS
The SUS has the following strengths:

- The SUS is free.
- It can be used on software applications, mobile apps, hardware, consumer products, and other types of systems.
- Multiple aspects of usability are covered.
- The analysis is simple.
- You can create subscales of usability and learnability (Sauro, 2011).
- It provides reasonably reliable results (Sauro, 2011; Tullis & Stetson, 2004).
- The SUS has received positive feedback from researchers (Sauro, 2011).

Weaknesses of the SUS
The SUS has the following weaknesses:

- Because it was designed for software applications, the SUS may need some modification for websites and web applications (Tullis & Stetson, 2004).
- Finstad (2006) found that 50% of nonnative English participants were not clear on the meaning of "cumbersome" in item 8 of the SUS. Changing "cumbersome" to "cumbersome/awkward" was suggested as a way to improve understandability for nonnative English speakers.
- The alternating of positive and negative words may result in errors. Sauro (2011) created a version of the SUS that used all positive phrasing and found comparable results with fewer errors.

Procedures for Administering the SUS
The SUS questionnaire is given to participants after they have had some experience with a particular system, for example, at the end of a usability test or after they use a system during a beta test in the field. Participants are asked to check the extent to which they agree or disagree with each statement. Participants are asked to check every item, and if they feel like an item does not quite apply, to check the middle response, the number "3."

The generic nature of the SUS questionnaire makes it applicable to a wide variety of products, including hardware, software, and websites. Tullis and Stetson (2004), for example, used the SUS to assess the usability of two websites simply by changing the word "system" in the 10 statements to "website."

Data Analysis of the SUS Questionnaire

Scoring the SUS questionnaire is simple. The scores for each item range from 0 to 4 with 4 being the most positive score. To prevent a response bias, Brooke included both positive and negative statements in the SUS. Half the items in the SUS are phrased positively (1, 3, 5, 7, and 9). The score for each of these positive items is the rating minus 1 so if you rated item 1 as agree (4), then the score for that item would be 4−1 or 3. The other items (2, 4, 6, 8, and 10) are phrased negatively, so the score for each of these items would be 5 minus the rating. For example, if you rated item 10 as a 3, then the actual score would be 5−3 or 2.

To obtain the overall score on the SUS, you add up the values (making sure you have corrected for the use of negative and positive items) and multiply the sum of the scores by 2.5 (this is done to create a 0−100 scale). Table A.3 gives the calculation of the overall score from a single participant.

In Table A.3, a score of 77.5 indicates that the system is perceived as moderately usable by this participant. The final SUS score for a product is the average of the individual SUS scores from all of the respondents.

If you modify the SUS to have only positive statements as noted earlier, you do not reverse the scales.

Table A.3 Determining the Score of a Single Participant			
Item on SUS	Rating	Calculation	Score
1(+)	3	3 − 1	2
2(−)	2	5 − 2	3
3(+)	4	4 − 1	3
4(−)	3	5 − 3	2
5(+)	5	5 − 1	4
6(−)	1	5 − 1	4
7(+)	4	4 − 1	3
8(−)	1	5 − 1	4
9(+)	4	4 − 1	3
10(−)	2	5 − 2	3
		Sum of scores	31
		Sum × 2.5	77.5

Reliability, Validity, and Related Issues

Tullis and Stetson (2004) conducted a study that compared different questionnaires on their ability to reliably distinguish two different websites for different sample sizes. SUS fared well in the Tullis and Stetson study; SUS reliably distinguished between two different sites for sample sizes ranging from 8 to 14.

Jeff Sauro, an expert in the use of statistics in usability, published a book on the SUS (Sauro, 2011) in which he reports that the SUS is both reliable and valid based on multiple studies.

ASQ, CSUQ, and PSSUQ

Lewis (1995) developed a set of three questionnaires that can be used at different times during usability evaluations. The After Scenario Questionnaire (ASQ) was designed to collect usability feedback immediately after a task and has only three questions. The three ASQ items present the user with a set of statements and 7-point disagree/agree scales. Table A.4 gives the three items in a web-based version of the ASQ. Users can include notes related to each statement.

The Post Study System Usability Questionnaire (PSSUQ) was designed to be used at the end of a usability evaluation. The CSUQ is a variation of the PSSUQ designed for use in field studies and surveys rather than usability laboratory tests. Perlman (n.d., http://www.acm.org/ ~ perlman/question.html) provides a web-based customizable script for creating surveys based on several "standard" questionnaires, including the ASQ (http://www.acm.org/perlman/question.cgi?form = ASQ) and the CSUQ (http://www.acm.org/perlman/question.cgi?form = CSUQ).

Table A.4 ASQ Statements and Rating Scales (Sauro & Lewis, 2012)			1	2	3	4	5	6	7		NA
1	Overall, I am satisfied with how easy it is to use this system	Strongly agree	o	o	o	o	o	o	o	Strongly disagree	o
2	Overall, I am satisfied with the amount of time it took to complete the tasks in this scenario	Strongly agree	o	o	o	o	o	o	o	Strongly disagree	o
3	Overall, I am satisfied with the support information (online help, messages, documentation) when completing the tasks	Strongly agree	o	o	o	o	o	o	o	Strongly disagree	o
			1	2	3	4	5	6	7		

The PSSUQ is a 19-item questionnaire given at the end of a scenario-based laboratory evaluation. Like the ASQ, the PSSUQ presents users with a set of statements and 7-point disagree/agree scales.

Table A.5 gives the 19 questions of the PSSUQ (Lewis, 2002). Lewis notes that the PSSUQ is useful in competitive evaluations or when assessing changes in product usability as a function of iterative design changes during the development cycle (p. 486).

Procedures for Administering the ASQ, PSSUQ, and CSUQ
All three questionnaires use the common approach of presenting users with a statement (all positive here) and asking the users of a system to rate the level of agreement with the statement or indicate that the statement is not applicable. Users can enter specific comments for each item in the three questionnaires to provide specific examples or additional explanation.

Reliability, Validity, and Related Issues
The items in this set of questionnaires are all phrased positively, which could result in a response bias. This contrasts with the Software Usability Measurement Inventory (SUMI) and SUS questionnaires where there is a mix of negative and positive statements (http://www.ucc.ie/hfrg/baseline/questionnaires.html). Lewis (2002) discusses this problem and notes that negative statements create problems of interpretation and confusion that may be worse than a response bias from the positive statements in these three questionnaires.

Lewis (1991) reported that the ASQ scale score was sensitive enough to discriminate between different systems, users, and scenarios and had reasonably high reliability even though it was based on only three scales. Lewis correlated scores on the ASQ with success on task scenarios and found that there was a significant point-biserial correlation between success on task scenarios and positive ASQ ratings.

Lewis reported reliability values for the PSSUQ higher than 0.80 in his original work (Lewis, 1995) and his more recent work on the PSSUQ (Lewis, 2002). His recent work also provides evidence for

Table A.5 PSSUQ Statements and Rating Scale (Lewis, 2002, Appendix A)			1	2	3	4	5	6	7		NA
1	Overall, I am satisfied with how easy it is to use this system.	Strongly agree	o	o	o	o	o	o	o	Strongly disagree	o
2	It was simple to use this system.	Strongly agree	o	o	o	o	o	o	o	Strongly disagree	o
3	I could effectively complete the tasks and scenarios using this system.	Strongly agree	o	o	o	o	o	o	o	Strongly disagree	o
4	I was able to complete the tasks and scenarios quickly using this system.	Strongly agree	o	o	o	o	o	o	o	Strongly disagree	o
5	I was able to efficiently complete the tasks and scenarios using this system.	Strongly agree	o	o	o	o	o	o	o	Strongly disagree	o
6	I felt comfortable using this system.	Strongly agree	o	o	o	o	o	o	o	Strongly disagree	o
7	It was easy to learn to use this system.	Strongly agree	o	o	o	o	o	o	o	Strongly disagree	o
8	I believe I could become productive quickly using this system.	Strongly agree	o	o	o	o	o	o	o	Strongly disagree	o
9	The system gave error messages that clearly told me how to fix problems.	Strongly agree	o	o	o	o	o	o	o	Strongly disagree	o
10	Whenever I made a mistake using the system, I could recover easily and quickly.	Strongly agree	o	o	o	o	o	o	o	Strongly disagree	o
11	The information provided with this system (such as online help, on-screen messages, and other documentation) was clear.	Strongly agree	o	o	o	o	o	o	o	Strongly disagree	o
12	It was easy to find the information I needed.	Strongly agree	o	o	o	o	o	o	o	Strongly disagree	o
13	The information provided for the system was easy to understand.	Strongly agree	o	o	o	o	o	o	o	Strongly disagree	o
14	The information was effective in helping me complete the tasks and scenarios.	Strongly agree	o	o	o	o	o	o	o	Strongly disagree	o
15	The organization of information on the system screens was clear.	Strongly agree	o	o	o	o	o	o	o	Strongly disagree	o
16	The interface of this system was pleasant.	Strongly agree	o	o	o	o	o	o	o	Strongly disagree	o
17	I liked using the interface of this system.	Strongly agree	o	o	o	o	o	o	o	Strongly disagree	o
18	This system has all the functions and capabilities I expect it to have.	Strongly agree	o	o	o	o	o	o	o	Strongly disagree	o
19	Overall, I am satisfied with this system.	Strongly agree	o	o	o	o	o	o	o	Strongly disagree	o
			1	2	3	4	5	6	7		

convergent validity; that is, the PSSUQ correlates highly with other measures of user satisfaction ($p = 0.80$).

Data Analysis of the ASQ, PSSUQ, and CSUQ

The three scales in the ASQ can be summed to create a single scale, which makes for easier interpretation and analysis of the results (Lewis, 1991).

The PSSUQ, which is given at the end of a laboratory-based usability evaluation, and the CSUQ, which can be used online or in the field, have four scales with each item in a scale having the same weight (Lewis, 2002):

- *Overall usability*: Average the responses from participants to items 1 through 19.
- *System use*: Average the responses from participants to items 1 through 8.
- *Information quality*: Average the responses from participants to items 9 through 15.
- *Interface quality*: Average the responses to items 16 through 18.

Where Do You Go to Find ASQ, PSSUQ, and CSUQ?

Perlman (n.d.) has created a website that allows you to create web versions of ASQ and CSUQ: http://www.acm.org/~perlman/question. html. The two papers by Lewis (1995, 2002) also provide details on the three questionnaires.

Microsoft Product Reaction Cards

Benedek and Miner (2002) developed a set of 118 positive and negative words (Table A.6) that can be used to assess user reactions to products or compare a product team's perception of the product against the perceptions of different user groups. Permission is granted to use this tool for personal, academic, and commercial purposes. If you wish to use this tool, or the results obtained from the use of this tool for personal or academic purposes or in your commercial application, you are required to include the following attribution: "Developed by and © 2002 Microsoft Corporation. All rights reserved."

Procedures for Administering the Microsoft Product Reaction Cards

Each word in Table A.6 is written on a separate card. After using a product in a usability test, each participant is asked to select a set of terms (as few or as many as the participant wanted) that best described

Table A.6 List of 118 Positive and Negative Words for the Microsoft Product Reactions Cards

Accessible	Creative	Fast	Meaningful	Slow
Advanced	Customizable	Flexible	Motivating	Sophisticated
Annoying	Cutting edge	Fragile	Not secure	Stable
Appealing	Dated	Fresh	Not valuable	Sterile
Approachable	Desirable	Friendly	Novel	Stimulating
Attractive	Difficult	Frustrating	Old	Straightforward
Boring	Disconnected	Fun	Optimistic	Stressful
Business-like	Disruptive	Gets in the way	Ordinary	Time-consuming
Busy	Distracting	Hard to use	Organized	Time-saving
Calm	Dull	Helpful	Overbearing	Too technical
Clean	Easy to use	High quality	Overwhelming	Trustworthy
Clear	Effective	Impersonal	Patronizing	Unapproachable
Collaborative	Efficient	Impressive	Personal	Unattractive
Comfortable	Effortless	Incomprehensible	Poor quality	Uncontrollable
Compatible	Empowering	Inconsistent	Powerful	Unconventional
Compelling	Energetic	Ineffective	Predictable	Understandable
Complex	Engaging	Innovative	Professional	Undesirable
Comprehensive	Entertaining	Inspiring	Relevant	Unpredictable
Confident	Enthusiastic	Integrated	Reliable	Unrefined
Confusing	Essential	Intimidating	Responsive	Usable
Connected	Exceptional	Intuitive	Rigid	Useful
Consistent	Exciting	Inviting	Satisfying	Valuable
Controllable	Expected	Irrelevant	Secure	
Convenient	Familiar	Low maintenance	Simplistic	

the product or how he or she felt about the product. The facilitator leaves the room while the person selects a set of words. When the participant is finished, the facilitator comes back into the room, records the cards chosen by the participant, and then asks the participant to choose the five "best" cards—the cards that best describe the participant's reactions to the product. The facilitator then interviews the participants about why they chose their five best cards.

Reliability, Validity, and Related Issues
Limited information is available on the reliability and validity of the Product Reaction Card method. Tullis and Stetson (2004) found, with small samples, that this method showed a significant difference in user preferences for two financial websites (as did the other four

questionnaires in their study: SUS, QUIS, CSUQ, and a Fidelity Usability Questionnaire). However, they also noted that the Product Reaction Card method yielded the most variability.

Where Do You Go to Find Microsoft Product Reaction Cards?
You can find the list of 118 words for the Product Reaction Cards at http://www.microsoft.com/usability/UEPostings/ProductReaction Cards.doc.

Data Analysis for Microsoft Product Reaction Cards
You can examine the data from a Product Reaction Card study in several ways:

- Ask different groups (developers versus users) to choose the cards that describe a product and then compare the patterns of words.
- Compare the five "best" cards across user groups or competitive products.
- Ask a group (or groups) to choose words that describe their reactions to a set of competitive products and compare whether there is overlap or any general patterns. Does one product stand out as more "desirable" than another based on the ratio of positive to negative words used?
- Examine the percentage of positive versus negative words by counting up the number of positive words chosen by participants and dividing by the total number of positive and negative words. For example, if a participant chooses 15 cards with 10 positive words and 5 negative words, then you would have a "score" of $(10/15) \times 100$ or 67%.

QUIS™: The Questionnaire for User Satisfaction
QUIS was developed at the Human−Computer Interaction Laboratory at the University of Maryland (Chin, Hiehl, & Norman, 1988; Harper & Norman, 1993; Harper, Slaughter, & Norman, 1997, November). The purpose of QUIS is to assess subjective satisfaction with a set of human−computer factors, including terminology, system feedback, features, documentation, installation, multimedia, and even virtual reality.

Procedures for Administering the QUIS Questionnaire
QUIS can be modified to suit the needs of a particular product. For example, you could eliminate the sections on installation and Internet access if those factors are not a concern for you. QUIS begins with a set of demographic questions, followed by six scales that deal with

overall system satisfaction, and 11 sections that deal with specific UI factors. Each statement in the survey is rated on a 9-point scale with a "not applicable" item if the particular item does not apply.

Data Analysis of the QUIS Questionnaire

The data from QUIS can be analyzed in many ways. One method described at the QUIS site (http://lap.umd.edu/QUIS/QuantQUIS.htm) involves creating a profile showing how each item in the questionnaire deviates from the overall mean. Then you select the items with the lowest values under the assumption that these are where the product has the most problems. This approach can indicate where the product has particular strengths and weaknesses. After you identify the items or areas with the lowest scores, you identify the flaws in the product that lead to low scores and consider solutions for each of those flaws.

Where Do You Go to Purchase QUIS?

Information on licensing of QUIS can be found at http://lap.umd.edu/QUIS/. The costs for QUIS range from $50 to $1000, depending on the class of user (student, academic/nonprofit, commercial) and whether you want the paper or web version.

Software Usability Measurement Inventory

SUMI is one of the most popular and well known of the commercial usability questionnaires. This questionnaire, now available in 11 languages, captures subjective usability or user satisfaction information by asking users to rate their agreement or disagreement with a set of 50 statements dealing with five aspects of product usability:

- Affect
- Efficiency
- Helpfulness
- Control
- Learnability

SUMI is generally used with a working prototype or an actual product. SUMI uses a 3-point Likert format with Agree, Undecided, and Disagree. Table A.7 gives an example of the style of the SUMI format.

Procedures for Administering the SUMI Questionnaire

The procedures for administering SUMI are simple. The questionnaire is generally administered immediately after a person has used a

Table A.7 Format of the SUMI		Agree	Undecided	Disagree
1	The software responds too slowly to inputs.	☐	☐	☐
2	I would recommend this software to my colleagues.	☐	☐	☐

product. Participants (a sample of at least 10 participants is generally recommended) are asked to check whether they agree or disagree with a set of 50 statements related to their experience with the product.

Reliability, Validity, and Related Issues
SUMI has been the object of numerous validity and reliability studies (Bevan, 1995; Kirakowski, n.d.) since the early 1990s. Details on research that focused on the validity and reliability of SUMI can be found at http://www.ucc.ie/hfrg/questionnaires/sumi/sumipapp.html#sumidev.

Data Analysis of the SUMI Questionnaire
SUMI provides a global score and scores on each of the five subscales listed earlier. The scores can be compared with a standardization database of results from other SUMI studies. You could, for example, see how your product compares to other similar products.

Where Do You Go to Purchase SUMI?
The approximate cost of the SUMI is about $1200. Ordering information for SUMI is available at http://www.ucc.ie/hfrg/questionnaires/sumi/pricing.html.

Website Analysis and Measurement Inventory
Website Analysis and Measurement Inventory (WAMMI) is a questionnaire for assessing the usability of website (WAMMI, 2013). WAMMI can be used to get early feedback on how users might react to particular prototype designs, to monitor ongoing reactions to your website, and to compare one website with competing websites.

Data Analysis of the WAMMI
WAMMI (Kirakowski & Cierlik, 1998; Kirakowski & Claridge, 1998) reports provide an overall usability score, a profile that shows scores on separate usability attributes (attractiveness, controllability, efficiency, helpfulness, and learnability), text responses, cross-tabulations, and other custom analyses.

Reliability, Validity, and Related Issues

The WAMMI website provides data on reliability at http://www. wammi.com/reliability.html. The Global score has a reported reliability of 0.900 (Cronbach's Alpha). The WAMMI team notes that valid data can be obtained with as few as 40 representative users.

Where Do You Go to Find WAMMI?

Information on WAMMI can be found at http://www.wammi.com.

REFERENCES FOR WAMMI

Kirakowski, J., & Cierlik, B. (1998). *Measuring the usability of web sites.* Paper presented at the HFES annual conference, Chicago.

Kirakowski, J., & Claridge, N. (1998, June). *Human centered measures of success in web site design.* Paper presented at the fifth human factors and the Web meeting, Basking Ridge, NY.

WAMMI web site. Retrieved on June 4, 2013 from <http://www.wammi.com/ >.

REFERENCES FOR THE SUS

Brooke, J. (n.d.). SUS: A quick and dirty usability scale. Retrieved June 4, 2013 from <http://www.usabilitynet.org/trump/documents/Suschapt.doc>.

Brooke, J. (1996). SUS: A quick and dirty usability scale. In P. W. Jordan, B. Thomas, B. A. Weerdmeester, & I. L. McClelland (Eds.), *Usability evaluation in industry* (pp. 189−194). London: Taylor & Francis.

Finstad, K. (2006). The system usability scale and non-native English speakers. *Journal of Usability Studies, 1*(4), 185−188.

Sauro, J. (2011). *A practical guide to the system usability scale: Background, benchmarks, & best practices.* Denver, CO: Measuring Usability LLC.

Sauro, J., & Lewis, J. R. (2012). *Quantifying the user experience: Practical statistics for user research.* Waltham, MA: Morgan Kaufmann.

REFERENCES FOR ASQ, PSSUQ, AND CUSQ

Lewis, J. R. (1991). Psychometric evaluation of an after-scenario questionnaire for computer usability studies: The ASQ. *SIGCHI Bulletin, 23*(1), 78−81.

Lewis, J. R. (1995). IBM computer usability satisfaction questionnaires: Psychometric evaluation and instructions for use. *International Journal of Human−Computer Interaction, 7*(1), 57−78.

Lewis, J. R. (2002). Psychometric evaluation of the PSSUQ using data from five years of usability studies. *International Journal of Human−Computer Interaction, 14*(3,4), 463−488.

Sauro, J., & Lewis, J. R. (2012). *Quantifying the user experience: Practical statistics for user research.* Waltham, MA: Morgan Kaufmann.

REFERENCES FOR MICROSOFT PRODUCT REACTION CARDS

Benedek, J., & Miner, T. (2002). Measuring desirability: New methods for evaluating desirability in a usability lab setting. *Proceedings of UPA 2002 conference*. Orlando, FL, July 8–12, 2002.

Tullis, T. S., & Stetson, J. N. (2004). *A comparison of questionnaires for assessing website usability*. Paper presented at the usability professionals association annual conference, Minneapolis, MN: UPA. Available also at <http://home.comcast.net/~tomtullis/publications/UPA2004Tullis Stetson.pdf> Accessed 6.06.13. Fee-based surveys.

REFERENCES FOR QUIS

Chin, J. P., Hiehl, V. A., & Norman, K. L. (1988). Development of an instrument measuring user satisfaction of the human–computer interface: Interface evaluations. *Proceedings of ACM CHI'88 conference on human factors in computing systems* (pp. 213–218). Available online at <http://www.lap.umd.edu/QUIS/>.

Harper, B. D., & Norman, K. L. (1993). Improving user satisfaction: The Questionnaire for User Interaction Satisfaction Version 5.5. *Proceedings of the first annual mid-Atlantic human factors conference* (pp. 224–228). Virginia Beach, VA. Available online at <http://www.lap.umd.edu/QUIS/>.

Harper, B., Slaughter, L., & Norman, K. (1997, November). *Questionnaire administration via the WWW: A validation and reliability study for a user satisfaction questionnaire*. Paper presented at WebNet 97, Association for the Advancement of Computing in Education, Toronto, Canada. Available online at <http://www.lap.umd.edu/QUIS/>.

Sauro, J., & Lewis, J. R. (2012). *Quantifying the user experience: Practical statistics for user research*. Waltham, MA: Morgan Kaufmann.

REFERENCES FOR SUMI

Bevan, N. (1995). Measuring usability as quality of use. *Software Quality Journal, 4*, 115–150 Retrieved on June 4, 2013 from <http://www.usability.serco.com/papers/qusab95.pdf>.

Kirakowski (n.d.). SUMI website. Retrieved on June 4, 2013 from <http://www.ucc.ie/hfrg/questionnaires/sumi/index.html>.

Sauro, J., & Lewis, J. R. (2012). *Quantifying the user experience: Practical statistics for user research*. Waltham, MA: Morgan Kaufmann.